LAST COPY

ems should be returned on or before the last date
nown below. Items not already requested by other
orrowers may be renewed in person, in writing or by
elephone. To renew, please quote the number on the
arcode label. To renew online a PIN is requi
his can be requested at your local library.
enew

ine

Under
PRESSURE

Under
PRESSURE

How Playing Football

Almost Cost Me Everything

and Why I'd Do It All Again

Ray Lucas
with David Seigerman

TRIUMPH
B O O K S

This book is available in quantity at special discounts for your group or organization. For further information, contact:
Triumph Books LLC
814 North Franklin
Chicago, Illinois 60610
www.triumphbooks.com

Printed in U.S.A.

ISBN: 978-1-60078-960-1

Design by Sue Knopf

Photos courtesy of Ray Lucas unless otherwise indicated

I dedicate this book to my wife, Cecy, and my three beautiful daughters, Rayven, Madison, and Kayla.

Cecy, I've played with some very tough guys. But what you did for those years I was sick was amazing. No one I know is stronger or tougher than you are. You are my rock.

It is not the critic who counts: not the man who points out how the strong man stumbles or where the doer of deeds could have done better. The credit belongs to the man who is actually in the arena, whose face is marred by dust and sweat and blood, who strives valiantly, who errs and comes up short again and again, because there is no effort without error or shortcoming, but who knows the great enthusiasms, the great devotions, who spends himself in a worthy cause; who, at the best, knows, in the end, the triumph of high achievement, and who, at the worst, if he fails, at least fails while daring greatly, so that his place shall never be with those cold and timid souls who neither know victory nor defeat.

—Theodore Roosevelt
"Citizenship in a Republic" speech,
Paris, France, April 23, 1910

Contents

Foreword

I met Ray Lucas under a strange set of circumstances.

We talked first on the phone around 10:00 AM the day after the 1996 NFL Draft. I was the head coach of the New England Patriots at the time, and we had our first squad meeting at 5:00 PM that night in Boston. Somehow, he got up there from New Jersey in time—probably sooner than I expected. He was wearing a suit and tie, and he and I had a chance to sit down and talk, face to face, for about 15 minutes.

His head coach at Rutgers, Doug Graber, had a lot to do with me having that meeting. Doug and I weren't buddy-buddy, but I did have a lot of respect for him. He told me I needed to take a look at this guy, and when he says something, he means it. That got my attention.

So, Ray came into my office and told me that he felt he could be a quarterback, and that if he had to, he would go up to Canada and play quarterback to prove it. I told him, "Go ahead."

But I also told him that I thought I could find him a spot doing something for us. I didn't know what it would be, and

I couldn't guarantee him anything. But if he took me at my word, I'd figure it out.

"Ray," I said, "you're just gonna have to trust me."

He got up and took a little walk around the room. He walked around and around in a little eight-foot circle, thinking. Then he stopped, shook my hand, and said, "Let's go."

That impressed me. He didn't want to go to Canada. He knew it wasn't the best thing for his career at the time. He needed to give the NFL a shot first; he could always go to Canada later if things didn't work out.

I could sense something special about Ray right away. He had the kind of determination you look for in a football player. I just didn't know yet whether he'd be willing to pay the price to succeed. A lot of times, when a player finds out what he really has to do to make it in the NFL, the whole idea seems a lot less attractive.

But Ray was one of those special kids I took a liking to immediately. I really did. It gets personal with some of the players you have the opportunity to coach, and you really feel a little love in your heart for guys like Ray, especially when you see where he came from and what he was able to achieve. I really hold him in high regard.

Ray is quite an inspirational guy. He had some attributes that weren't visible to everybody. I'm not talking about as a quarterback; I had seen him play at Rutgers, and I knew his arm was a bit wild, that he tended to overthrow the ball. Everything about the way he played the position was violent.

But he had some rare leadership qualities. He was able to rally his teammates, even though he was an untested and unproven player. That's one of the things that impressed me the most. He could step into the huddle with a bunch of veteran players, without having really played much before, and command their respect. It takes a unique individual to get that done.

As time went on, we did figure things out, just like I told him we would. I saw that he was willing to sacrifice to get what he wanted, and he did every job I ever asked him to do. Whatever responsibility I gave him, he made me take notice. Then I'd think, *Maybe I could give this guy a little more.* So, I gave him this job and that job, and soon he had this little repertoire of things he could do.

He didn't escape all those things that players had to go through to earn my respect; he was right there in the middle of it. The players who are willing to do what he did are rare, unselfish individuals. His attitude was observed by other people in the organization, especially all the coaches, and he earned a lot of respect for what he did for us in New England.

The Jersey connection was probably big for us, too. He was used to hearing people like me, and I was used to hearing people like him. He and I spoke the same language. He's a real straightforward, in-your-face guy, and I liked that about him right from the start.

I remember one time later on when we were with the New York Jets, I introduced him to someone I knew who was working in the presidential cabinet. Ray had expressed an interest in working in law enforcement someday, and I was trying to help get him squared away for his future after football. I remember after that meeting, the guy told me, "This guy could run for office."

I have a lot of respect for Ray Lucas, for what he did and for all that he's been through. I just hope things continue to go well for him and his family.

—*Bill Parcells*

"I'm sorry, but we're in a fund-raising phase right now. Can you call back another time?"

And with that, I was done. My one last shot had been shot down.

I was finished, but first, I had to unload on this lady who had been unlucky enough to have picked up the phone. I hit her with everything that had been building up inside of me over the previous eight years. I cursed her and her family and everyone at that fucking group of hers that was raising funds supposedly so they could help guys exactly like me when a call exactly like this came. I screamed and cursed and cried. I had just told some stranger on the phone that I was going to kill myself, and she had reacted as if I'd just called to order a sandwich.

I hung up and looked around the shitty little one-bedroom apartment that the five of us were living in. It was the first place my wife, Cecy, and I could find when we had to sell our house, the home we had built for ourselves and our three children, just before Christmas. It was an apartment just a few steps from the bridge that connects Harrison to Newark in New Jersey, so close to the street that drunks would stumble into our front door all night long.

I shook my head, still trying to believe what I'd just heard.

"Can you call back another time?"

No. I couldn't. I was out of time.

And then the funniest thing happened: I felt calm. The pain in my neck went away. So did the pain in my back and in my knees. Gone. The fog I'd been in from all the pain pills I'd been swallowing lifted. I was no longer depressed. I felt no anxiety. I wasn't mad anymore.

For the first time in years, I had clarity.

Better. I had a plan.

The idea of killing myself was not a new one. I had already been having that debate with the voice in my head, the one that was always telling me, *Look at yourself. You're filthy. You smell. You're an embarrassment. You're worthless. You're not helping anyone. You're a burden. You need to kill yourself.*

For a while, I would think of reasons to argue with that voice.

"I'm a father."

You're a fucking joke.

"I'm a husband."

You should kill yourself because of what you're doing to your wife.

Eventually, getting from "Look what you've become" to "How are you going to do it?" becomes a pretty short walk.

So, you start to figure out a way. You listen to the voice.

Try the pills.

Made sense. I had enough of them around. When you take 1,400 pills a month, there was always a potentially lethal dose handy.

There was still some small part of me saying, "Are you listening to yourself? What the hell are you doing?"

But that was way in the background. People always talk about having a good angel and a bad angel. Well, my bad angel was kicking the shit out of my good angel on a daily basis. As soon as I'd hear a whisper from the good one, the bad one would stab him with a pitchfork.

Try the pills.

So one night, before I went to sleep, I took 50 pain pills.

The next morning, I woke up. I don't know how, but I woke up.

The good angel tried a little harder to get my attention: "What are you doing? What happens to the girls after you're gone?"

But that other voice was louder.

Tonight, take 60.

So, I took 60 pills the next night.

And the next morning, I woke up.

You are fucking pathetic. You can't even kill yourself right.

Maybe it was that other little voice that convinced me to make that last call for help. Clearly, that didn't turn out too well.

But now, at least, I had a plan. Something I could actually look forward to.

It came together so easily. It made sense. I'd kill myself on Sunday.

I actually sat there in the kitchen thinking about it and smiling. It was perfect. Cecy and our three daughters would leave for church. I'd write the note, get in my truck, and go.

Right then and there, alone, in that shitty kitchen, I felt at peace. It was going to be over, and I could hardly wait.

Thank God this is going to be over, I thought to myself. *I can't do this anymore. I can't be a drain on my wife and kids anymore. I'm not doing anything to help support them. I'm not there for them when they need me. I'm a ghost. I just can't wait for the pain to go away.*

That was it. A minute or two after I'd hung up the phone, I had clarity, a plan, and a date.

It was a Wednesday. Four days later, on Sunday morning, when my family went to church, to pray for me to get better, I finally was going to fix everything.

I was going to drive off the George Washington Bridge.

1

Get Off the Bus

My first NFL concussion came on my first NFL play.

I was the worst wide receiver on the New England Patriots roster. The worst. I was brutal. But I was out there on the field in Green Bay, covering the opening kickoff of our first game of the 1996 preseason.

Back then, the NFL had yet to outlaw the wedge. That's when three or four fatties would line up shoulder to shoulder or hold hands or lock their arms together and form a wall in front of the kick returner. The first player on the kicking team to the wedge had to split it.

I was lined up as R3—third guy from the outside, right side of the formation—and started running down the field with the rest of the kick coverage team. I looked to my left and didn't see anybody. I looked to my right. Nobody. I realized, *I'm out in front. I have to bust the wedge.*

I watched the wedge come together, and it gave me the slightest pause as I considered for the first time what was about to happen. For a split second, I thought, *Oh shit*. And then it was gone. Instead of getting scared, a switch flipped. I went crazy and picked up speed. It was my first NFL play, and I was going to kill every son of a bitch in that wall.

To split the wedge, you had to hit it right in the middle. If you hit it from the outside, you've taken yourself out of the play. The blockers are like bowling pins, and you have to separate the two in the middle. That's not so easy to do. You can't leave your feet or it's a penalty. You can't go low to take them out. Penalty. Basically, you're fucked. Which is why they eventually got rid of the wedge. But not before I had to go split it, full speed, right down the middle, which is what I did.

A few seconds later, I woke up on my back, looking up at the sky from the turf of Lambeau Field. I had knocked myself completely unconscious and had no idea what had happened after impact. I simply got up, saw guys in the huddle, and figured, *That's where I need to be.*

So, I walked over and joined the Green Bay Packers huddle.

I looked around at everyone, not recognizing any faces or having a clue what was going on. Brett Favre noticed me and laughed, then started waving over at our sideline and yelled, "You better come get your boy."

When I got to our sideline, Bill Parcells came right over to me.

"What the fuck is wrong with you?"

"Nothing."

"Are you all right?"

"Yeah. I'm good."

And that was that. The trainers came over and asked me if I was all right. I told them the same thing: "Yeah. I'm good." That was pretty much the extent of a concussion test back in the mid-1990s.

No one even called them concussions. They were "burners" on offense, "stingers" on defense. Sometimes, they were "dings." Call them whatever you want but they were all the same thing: concussions. Your brain had just been bounced around inside your skull.

When it happens, you feel like warm water is sliding down one side of your head. You usually can't hear anything in one ear, or if you do hear a sound, it's like a faint ringing. You can't see straight, so you close one eye and try to focus. If that doesn't work, you close the other eye and see if that works any better. You do that for 40 seconds, the trainer comes over, asks you if you're all right, and you say, "Yeah. I'm good."

I finished my football career with about 20 burners, and the one in Green Bay wasn't my first. The first one came my sophomore season at Rutgers, when we were playing at West Virginia, my first full year as starting quarterback. They had a safety named David Mayfield, who had been considered one of the bigger hitters in the Big East that year. We were running a sprint pass, and I never saw Mayfield; he was out of my sight line when I made the throw. My receiver was running a hook, and Mayfield stepped right in and intercepted it, but not cleanly. He was juggling it at first, and my immediate reaction was that I needed to go separate him from the ball.

I ran at him, and when we were a yard or two apart, we looked right into each other's eyes. We both knew what was coming. I hit him, spun around, and was out cold.

I didn't know until later, after I'd seen it on film, that after I'd made the hit I spun around and stood right in the path of some defensive lineman, who came out of nowhere and sent me flying through the air.

When I got up from the hit, the training staff was there, ready to ask me that all-important question.

"Are you all right?"

"Yeah, yeah, yeah."

I guess they could tell that I wasn't, because they followed up with some more probing questions.

"Do you know where you are?"

"Yeah."

"Where are you?"

"Yeah."

"What's your name?"

"Yeah."

"What day is it?"

"Yeah."

It was pretty bad. We wound up getting crushed 58–22, and on the plane ride home, I asked the guy sitting next to me, "Are we on our way to the game?"

He immediately hit the overhead call button, and the team doctors came over to ask me more questions. But that was it. No big deal. Just a burner. At some point during the flight home, the fog lifted, the ringing in my ears stopped, and everything was back to normal. And I was right back in the lineup the next week at Miami.

Shortly after that opening kickoff concussion in Green Bay, we were flying home from another preseason game. All the rookies sat together on the plane, and one of the offensive linemen turned to me and asked, "Are we on our way to the game?"

So it was my turn to start banging the buzzer, calling over the team doctors, and laughing my ass off now that I was on the other end of the conversation.

• • •

I hadn't planned on playing special teams or wide receiver in the NFL. I was a quarterback. But I would have done anything in the world for the chance to keep playing football after college. If Parcells had told me after practice to go shine the helmets, they would have been the shiniest, sexiest helmets you've ever seen.

I didn't have a lot of choices coming out of Rutgers. It was the era of the pocket quarterback, and there weren't too many guys in the league who were doing what I was doing in college—running around, keeping plays alive with my legs the way Russell Wilson and Robert Griffin III are doing today. I wasn't even invited to play in any of the postseason all-star showcase games, so I figured I wasn't going to get a chance at the NFL.

In fact, I had already decided to start playing basketball for Rutgers. Growing up, I actually loved basketball more than football. Every time my mother sent me to the store to buy cigarettes, I went with a basketball in my hand. I'd dribble right-handed on the way there, left-handed on the way back. I scored 2,198 points as a point guard in high school and went to Howard Garfinkel's Five-Star Camp three years in a row. Once, we had Rick Pitino as a guest speaker. During his talk, he brought out Billy McCaffrey (who went on to be one of the top scorers on Duke's 1991 title team) and me to demonstrate how to shoot the basketball. I took double recruiting visits to Syracuse and Virginia, and could have played football or basketball in college.

I chose Rutgers and football. But when my final football season ended, I talked with Bob Wenzel, the basketball coach, about playing for him. I was all set to return to the court when my mother called me from home, saying she had received a letter from the NFL, inviting me to the scouting combine.

That was it for basketball. I dropped everything and started training for the combine.

I went to Indianapolis and worked out with the quarterbacks. I threw the ball pretty well, though I didn't enjoy the whole meat-market aspect of the combine. But the worst part of the process for me by far was the physical. The doctors wanted to see how my rotator cuff had healed after I'd had it reconstructed following my junior season.

That probably was my first real injury. We were playing Miami at home—it was our first big game in Rutgers' new football stadium, and I remember Warren Sapp coming out and kicking the pylons. In the third quarter, Sapp wrapped me up, drove me into the ground, and separated my shoulder.

I don't know how I did it but I played the rest of the season with a tear in my right rotator cuff. When I would bring my arm back to throw, it was fine. But when I started to come forward with the ball, it was a level of pain I had never experienced before. It was the kind of pain that brought tears to my eyes and left me blinking just to clear my vision. We're talking blinding pain on every fucking throw.

It didn't just hurt when I was throwing—my shoulder hurt constantly. I couldn't sleep, couldn't drive, couldn't lift anything. Most of the time, I would just let my arm hang there, resting on my stomach. I didn't even realize I was doing it until people came up to me and asked, "Hey, Luke, what's the matter with your arm?"

Still, the notion of sitting out never crossed my mind. None of us thought that way. Even in college, I always had teammates who played with injuries they probably shouldn't have been playing with. One of my linemen once came into the huddle with one of his fingers sticking out from the middle knuckle at a 90-degree angle. I just stared at it until he asked me, "What are you looking at?"

I said, "Dude, look at your finger."

He looked down and said, "Oh, shit." Just like that, the same way he would've sounded if he'd just realized he'd forgotten his car keys. No big deal. Just a finger pointing in the wrong direction. I was ready to throw up, but he just went to the sideline, and before the next play, he was back in the huddle, staring me in the face. He said, "It came out of the joint, so they just squeezed it back together. Let's go."

That, essentially, is the mentality of a football player. There's a difference between being hurt and being injured: hurt you can play, injured you can't. No one is going to admit he's injured unless he absolutely has to, so you play hurt without thinking twice. If you can't play with pain, you can't stay on the field. If you can't stay on the field, you can't stay in the NFL.

I played the rest of that college season with a tear in my rotator cuff, and we did the surgery the day after the season ended. Then I really found out was pain was. You can live with the bumps and bruises, but when they cut your shoulder wide open, drill holes, tie knots, and put in screws—that's real pain.

Fortunately, I healed fast—always have—and I was ready in time for camp. I didn't miss a beat my whole senior season. I hadn't worried about the shoulder at all until I met the doctor at the combine.

"How's your shoulder?" he asked me. "Does it hurt?"

"No."

"Well, it's gonna hurt today."

He proceeded to try and rip my shoulder out of the socket. He pulled it, twisted it, and moved it in every direction a shoulder is supposed to go—and some that it wasn't. The guy was kneeling on top of me with all of his weight, trying to see if he could roll my shoulder out of the socket. I passed the physical, but I was sore as shit the next day.

The only positive thing about my combine experience was one conversation that gave me some hope of getting drafted. It was with one of the coaches from the Pittsburgh Steelers, which made sense. Kordell Stewart had been with them for a couple of seasons by then, though he hadn't seen much time at quarterback. The guy asked me, "Can you do what he does?"

"Absolutely."

I thought I might end up a Steeler.

There weren't a lot of quarterbacks selected in the 1996 draft. Tony Banks was the first one off the board; he went 42nd to the Rams. The Eagles took Bobby Hoying at No. 85. Jeff Lewis went to Denver, Danny Kanell to the Giants.

And when Pittsburgh was on the clock with the 203rd pick, I was watching the graphic across the bottom of the screen on ESPN. I saw the pick—Spence Fischer, quarterback from Duke—flash onto the screen, and that was it. Eight quarterbacks wound up getting drafted. I wasn't one of them.

After the draft, my agent told me the Jacksonville Jaguars were interested in having me come down as an undrafted free agent. I told him to set it up, right away. An hour later, he told me that the Jaguars had invited South Carolina quarterback Steve Taneyhill instead. I fired my agent.

I woke up the morning after the draft thinking I'd just go back to school, finish my classes, and graduate. Even my backup, Robert Higgins, had been invited to San Diego's rookie camp. I hadn't heard anything from anyone.

But I had an idea.

When you go to the combine, you wind up taking home all kinds of business cards from coaches you meet from all over the league. I found the card for Mike Pope, who was the tight ends coach in New England. I called Mike and told him I needed to talk to Coach Parcells.

I had met Bill Parcells a few times when his teams practiced at Rutgers. I doubted he would remember me, but I had to take the shot. Mike transferred my call and when Parcells picked up, I started my sales pitch.

"Just give me a shot. Let me come up there and show you what I can do."

He listened for a minute or so and said, "Okay, kid."

I didn't know at the time I'd been recommended to him by Doug Graber, my head coach at Rutgers. Still, my call worked. Just like that, I was on my way to New England for rookie minicamp.

I spent my first day there as a wide receiver, even though I had never played receiver before. I was out there alongside Terry Glenn, who the Patriots had drafted over the weekend with the seventh overall pick.

I was awful.

After practice, we were on the bus for the one-mile drive back to the facility. I got called off the bus and needed to catch a ride back with one of the coaches.

That's it, I thought. *I'm going to get cut on the first day without even getting to take a shower.*

Parcells didn't cut me. But the second day, he had me practicing as a defensive back. I was out there alongside the team's second-round pick from that draft, Lawyer Milloy.

Again, we all started boarding the bus after practice, and, again, I got called off.

After the third practice—which I spent as a quarterback—I made a beeline for the back row, making it as hard as possible for them to find me and call me off the bus again. Sure enough, offensive coordinator Charlie Weis got on, came straight to the back, and said, "Get off the bus. Coach Parcells wants to talk to you."

I left the bus, figuring it would be for the last time. I got into Parcells' car for a ride back to the stadium and prepared myself for the worst.

"We want to keep you, if you want to stay," he said.

I wasn't quite sure I'd heard him correctly, so I asked him what he meant.

"It means we want to sign you. Do you have an agent?"

"No, but I'll sign any papers you have right now."

"You can't do that, Ray. You gotta get somebody to look at the contract."

To be honest, I didn't care what the contract said. I was signing it. Then he told me they would give me a signing bonus: $2,500. To me, it may as well have been $25,000. Give me the papers and show me where to sign.

When I flew home that night, I had on all the free Patriots stuff they gave me. I boarded the plane, wearing my new Patriots T-shirt and my new Patriots hat. A woman asked me, "Excuse me, are you a New England Patriot?" I just lost it. I started crying, I was so proud. I couldn't even squeak out a "Yes."

I came out of the airport and it seemed like everyone from my hometown of Harrison was there. It was an incredible feeling. I told my family and my friends, "I don't know what I'm doing and I don't know if I'm going to make it. But right now, I am on the team."

It probably didn't look that way at first. If you had watched one of our first practices that summer, you would have had a pretty good idea who should be the first player cut.

"Who is No. 15? That guy sucks. No way he makes the roster."

I would have agreed with you. I was playing wide receiver. And I really was terrible.

Learning how to run routes, figuring out the precision involved, was really difficult. Everything has to be done the right way at the right time or the whole thing doesn't work. Plus, I was going against Lawyer Milloy and Ty Law. It was a nightmare.

Early on, we were running a seven-on-seven drill, where the safeties were involved. The quarterback overthrew me on a slant. I went up and caught it, and Milloy hit me. Actually, it would be more accurate to say he nearly decapitated me.

I could barely breathe but I jumped up and glared right back at him anyway. He had no idea I had no air left in my lungs, and I wasn't about to let him know. I wanted him to take away a different message: "That ain't gonna get it done."

In my mind, though, I was thinking, *Oh my god, things are different up here.*

When you're a rookie, and you get smashed like that for the first time, you learn fast that you're not in Kansas anymore, Toto.

I held onto that ball, but I knew I was never going to make the team as a wide receiver.

I always heard Parcells stressing the importance of special teams and field position. He was always talking about the value of being versatile, that the more jobs you can do, the more guys it would take to replace you. I began to think that might be a way for me to slide onto the roster. There was absolutely no reason to think that would lead me to playing quarterback someday. There's not exactly a long history of guys who went from special teams to starting quarterback, but I sure as hell wasn't going to get there watching the games from my couch. So, I went to Mike Sweatman, the special teams coach, and told him, "Man, I have got to be on special teams."

His reaction wasn't encouraging: "You're out of your mind. Are you trying to get me fired?"

Sweatman wouldn't budge no matter how much I pleaded, so I needed a new approach. Every day, when the special teams were practicing, if I wasn't getting any attention from the coaches, I'd start a fight. I would literally start a fight with whoever I was lined up against, just to make sure everyone knew I was still out there.

One day, Parcells pulled me over and asked, "What is your fucking problem?"

"I'm just trying to catch your eye, Coach. Gotta do whatever I can."

He shook his head, "You fucking Jersey guys."

"And where are you from?" Of course, I knew the answer already. Hasbrouck Heights. About 12 miles from Harrison.

"Don't be a fucking wiseguy."

I must have gotten his attention, and he must have said something to Sweatman, because suddenly I was on the punt teams.

And I was a demon. I was making tackles and talking shit. One practice, I blocked two punts in a row. Sweatman wanted me to back off, but it was too late. I was already going 100 miles an hour. Nothing was going to stop me from giving them a reason to keep me on the roster. On the next snap, I pushed a guy right into punter Tom Tupa. And Parcells threw me out of practice.

Our practice field was about a mile away from our locker room. And even though most players were allowed to use golf carts, rookies didn't get that privilege. We had to walk.

I walked back alone. I had gotten all the way to the door when I heard a whistle. I turned around and it was—who else?—Parcells.

"You forgot something."

"What'd I forget?"

"All the wide receivers' pads and helmets."

So, I walked all the way back, picked up everyone's gear, and hauled it all back.

But that was a turning point for me. Finally, after all the years of getting hit, I was the one doing the hitting. And I kinda liked it. By the time we faced the Eagles in our third preseason game, I was making a strong case to stay on the roster.

I kept telling Sweatman, "Don't even bother telling me what you want me to do; I'm going after every single punt." In the first half, I just missed blocking two of them.

At halftime, I promised Sweatman that I was going to get one.

He got in my face: "I'm sick and fucking tired of you telling me what you're gonna do. Go block something."

In the second half, sure enough, I faked outside, got underneath, and blocked the punt. The ball bounced all the way down to the 1-yard line, and my feet were out of bounds when I picked it up to try to score with it. But it was my first big play—maybe big enough to win me a job.

I was also on the kickoff coverage unit, and during one return later in that game, I grabbed a blocker along the sideline, spun him around, and tossed him four feet out of bounds. As I came off the field, I heard Parcells say, "That's my homeboy right there."

That's when I knew I really had a chance.

When final cut day came, I wasn't sure what to expect. I'd been catching some balls, but I still wasn't good enough to make the team as just a receiver. If they were going to keep me around, it would be because of what I'd shown them on special teams. Had I done enough?

We came off the practice field, walked toward the building, and the Grim Reaper was there, standing right in front of the door. If he stopped you and sent you to see the coach, you were finished. Pack your bags, thanks for coming. I stopped and lagged behind for a few seconds, waiting for some of the big fatties to get in front of me, figuring I could sneak into the building behind them.

No such luck.

"Ray," the Reaper told me. "Coach Parcells wants to talk with you."

Shit.

When I got to his office, he was sitting at his desk, waiting for me.

"Listen, kid. I don't know what I'm going to do with you. I don't know what you can do for me. But we're going to put you on the practice squad."

I didn't know what that meant, so he explained that I would have to clear waivers, and once I did, I would be on the Patriots practice squad. Which meant I'd get to practice with the team but I wouldn't get to play in any games.

He told me that the salary for practice squad players was nowhere near the regular salary, but he said I'd be making $3,300 every two weeks.

To me, it sounded like the perfect arrangement. I was sold.

Whatever I needed to do to stick in the NFL, I was going to do. Happily.

2

Under the Annie Bridge

One of the first things Parcells told me when I got to rookie camp was that he doesn't treat everybody the same. He treats everyone *fairly*, but not the same.

"I have favorites," he told me on my first day. "You'll know who you are if you're a favorite. And you'll know it if you're not."

I think that's one of the reasons he and I meshed so well so fast. Bill Parcells is a no-nonsense guy. He will tell you like it is. If he told me it was going to rain, I'd go grab my umbrella.

He's a Jersey boy. And that means something to me.

Because I'm a Jersey boy.

Let's get one thing straight up front. We're not talking about the *Jersey Shore* shit; that's not real Jersey. People laugh at the image of New Jersey those people portrayed. Maybe one person on that show was actually from Jersey; the rest were from Staten Island or something. Just because they come here to hang out doesn't mean they're like us. That aggravated me, because that is not the world I grew up in.

I grew up in Harrison, one square mile just across the Passaic River from Newark, a couple miles south of the Meadowlands. When I grew up, I was the only dark spot in the whole town. There weren't any other black people here.

Not even my family.

My dad was away in the Navy, serving as a gunner in Vietnam, when my mom got pregnant. Dad came home, and on August 6, 1972, out popped the chocolate boy wonder. My dad stayed with my mom, and he raised me like his own.

My parents are white. My sister's white. When I was little, people would ask me if I was adopted; I had no idea what they were talking about.

"That's my mom, that's my dad, this is my family," I'd say. That was it.

When I got to grammar school at Holy Cross, race started to become an issue for some people. Older kids would block the doors at the end of the school day. If I could get to the exit, I didn't get beat up. If I got caught, I got beat up. I've always said I got my shakes running away from a lot of beatings. And there are only so many times you can get beat up before you learn how to fight back.

It wasn't always easy for my parents either. My dad worked two jobs, one as the executive director of a housing complex in town, the other as a bartender at a local restaurant, Cifelli's. When I was older, he told me about nights when guys would be drunk at the bar, asking him how he could stand to be raising me. How he could stay with my mom. More than once, they told him he ought to get that nigger out of his house.

My dad wouldn't say anything. He'd just keep pouring the drinks. And at the end of the night, when those guys walked out back to the parking lot, my dad went out and did what he had to do.

Years later, when I started playing sports, and I was all-state in football, basketball, and baseball, those same guys were still coming into the bar. Only now they'd ask my dad, "Hey Tommy, how's Ray doing? Tell him we said hi."

Sports meant everything in Harrison, and they became everything to me. Sports bridged the gap between me and everyone else. Suddenly, I wasn't looked at as the only black kid around. I was accepted. I found friends—the same guys that are my best friends today. My friend card has been full since I was five years old.

For the most part, I met them all through sports. Rec leagues, school sports, Pop Warner. Playing sports was the perfect place for a kid like me to build confidence and gain respect. Where a kid like me could belong.

The coaches we had back then were different than the guys we see today, even in Pop Warner. One practice when I was in the senior division, I was running a sweep and I ran out of bounds. My coach grabbed my facemask and started yelling at me, "What the hell are you doing? We don't run out of bounds here. You run into somebody."

He sent me back out and we ran sweep after sweep. Sweep right. Sweep left. Five in a row. Ten in a row. They taught us to play to the whistle. And we learned to be tough.

How could we not? Our Pop Warner coaches were all police officers.

Back then, when you screwed up at practice, your coach would get right up in your grill. Or he'd drag you by your facemask for 20 yards. Then, when you got home, your father would kick your ass because he'd been sitting in the stands watching practice, and you embarrassed him.

That lesson carried right up through high school. Our coaches would kick our asses at practice. Literally. I had one coach who kept telling me that when I ran out of the pocket, I should make sure not to throw the ball late. And the next time I did it, he promised, he'd kick my ass. Next game, I ran out of the pocket, threw it late, and when I got to the sideline, he actually tried to kick me in the ass.

Sometimes, the coaches would gather us up and play Bull in the Ring—which probably has been outlawed by now. They would put one guy in the middle of a ring of teammates, then call a name from someone in the circle. That guy would go in and hit the first guy. Some of us hit harder than others, and you knew how much trouble the "bull" was in by whose name the coaches would call. Things got really bad when they'd call four names at once, and they'd all rush in and smack the guy. Every one of us knew that at any given practice, it could be our turn in the ring. The one the coaches were trying to see if they would toughen up. Or break.

All of that made us hard as bricks. Mentally and physically. We had T-shirts that we wore everywhere, with two words on them: FAMILY and HIT. That was everything you needed to know about who we were and what we did. That was Harrison football.

And nobody wanted to come to play in Harrison.

Our high school stadium was bordered on one side by a lumber yard, a steel mill on another, and the Passaic River. The middle of the football field had no grass; it was pretty much all rocks. You could see it in the eyes of other teams when they got off the bus. Doubt. Nervousness. Fear. We had them beat the minute they showed up.

You knew that when you came to Harrison, you were probably going to need a little extra ice for the ride back home. We hit everything that moved. We never backed down from anybody. Some people said we were dirty—but after getting the shit kicked out of you for four years, what else are you going to say?

One time, we were playing Carlstadt–East Rutherford, and their quarterback also played safety. I was running the ball, got past the linebackers, and broke into the secondary. He was coming toward me on an angle, and instead of continuing to run toward the sideline, I cut back and started running right at him. I hit him at full speed and we both went down. I jumped right up and looked down on him, lying there. He looked at me for a second, then he looked away. I knew right then and there, this guy was fucking finished.

We learned through football that together—11 guys, all doing what they're supposed to be doing—we are strong. Separate, selfish, we're all weakened. As soon as one guy starts doing his own thing, it all breaks down. That couldn't be accepted. Not by coaches, not by the players.

It was a lesson I learned early on growing up in Harrison: the weak sink.

That's why sometimes things had to be settled in The Pit. There was an area right outside the coaches' office, behind the stands, cut off from view of everyone in the stadium. If two guys had a disagreement, they'd be directed to take their helmets off and go work it out in The Pit. No one ever backed down. If anyone had ever said, "Nah, I don't want to go to The Pit," forget it—it would have been over for him. End of the road. That's how it is in Jersey. Once you lose the respect of a Jersey boy, you will never get it back. Ever.

Respect was huge in my house. It was my father's way. When I was a kid, I wouldn't walk around town, cussing up a storm with my friends. Someone would hear us, and it would be a direct reflection on my father. He wouldn't stand for us embarrassing him that way.

One time, I ran off to play basketball. On my way to the park, I bounced the ball off a bus and just kept on my way, running over to the courts. I played for three hours, came home, and my father was waiting.

"Come have a seat."

I had no idea what I'd done wrong.

"If I ever hear about you doing something like that again…"

Somehow, he found out about the bus. Somebody saw it, told my father, and that almost cost me a major ass-kicking. He wanted things done the right way, and I came to respect that. I still take Navy showers the way he taught me to when I was 11: get wet under the water, shut the water off, soap up, turn the water on, rinse quickly, then squeeze the water off your body.

Respect. Discipline. Toughness. That's the Jersey I grew up in.

When I was younger and went to watch Harrison football games, I couldn't wait to be part of that world. Not just the games, but all of it.

Then, when I was a freshman, playing running back on the JV team, Mickey Rowe, the starting quarterback on varsity, got hurt. This guy was my idol. He was doing exactly what I dreamed of doing. He won a state championship as a junior, and here he was, as a senior, getting ready to go visit all these big-time colleges. Then, he breaks his leg. Next thing I know, they moved me up to varsity, and I'm riding the bus with all the guys I absolutely idolized.

I came up and couldn't wait to get hazed. The varsity guys would shave your head, and I loved it. It was a rite of passage. A sign that you belonged to the team.

Suddenly, not only was I a part of the program, I was on varsity. As a freshman.

Only varsity players got to wear their jerseys around school the day before a game. I didn't care that, at first, they gave me a jersey with somebody else's number on it. It was some Polish kid, and I'd be out on the field, playing defense, and you'd hear the P.A. guy announce, "Tackle by Sudziarski." I know everyone in the stadium was looking around, thinking, "What kind of black guy is named Sudziarski?" Didn't matter to me. I was out there, playing for Harrison.

Soon enough, they started to give me some snaps at quarterback, only because I had a rocket for an arm. I could throw a ball through a wall. They would bring me into the game and call a Go route. Basically, they'd send the receiver deep, have me drop back as far as I could, and then I'd throw it downfield as far as I could.

I loved it. Especially when I was a sophomore and I became the starting quarterback. When you're the quarterback, you're the Chief. Everyone else is an Indian. And when Chief's talking in the huddle, no one else says a word. Sometimes, I would be in the huddle, calling a play, looking into the faces of the guys I used to sit in the stands and dream about playing with. And here they were, all listening to me. It was amazing.

We did everything together. When you're on varsity, you got to hang out under the "Annie Bridge." That's the bridge they used at the end of the 1982 movie *Annie*; an old, abandoned railroad bridge that crosses the Passaic River. And it's where all the older high school kids would go drink. Jocks, burnouts, everyone would be down there. Getting to hang out with seniors at the Annie Bridge, being accepted as one of them, was about as prestigious an honor as I could imagine. To be in a world that I had dreamed about was incredible. It was a long damn way from running for the exits at Holy Cross.

Sometimes, we would take the ride up Passaic Avenue, through Kearny and up to the Dunkin' Donuts in North Arlington. Now *that* was a rivalry. A bench-clearing brawl with North Arlington was like a Thanksgiving tradition for us. It was never a matter of whether it would happen, only when.

We would hop in someone's car and drive up to North Arlington in our Harrison jackets, collars up, BLUE TIDE emblazoned on the back. And all those championship patches. We'd go see if anyone had the balls to come over and say anything to us.

Even when I was a freshman, I knew what it meant to be in that car. When you took the drive to Dunkin' Donuts, where cars would be four-deep in the parking lot, you better be ready to throw hands. If you weren't ready to fight when you got to North Arlington, you better be ready to fight your teammates on the drive back.

That's how it was. We went everywhere together. We did everything together. We were family.

Our coaches referred to us as "The Boys," and if you messed with one of the boys, you were messing with all of us. Together strong. Separate weak. One die, all die.

That's what it means to be from Harrison. To be from Jersey.

It's where I learned I had to be tougher than everybody else. It's where I learned to be a quarterback. And it's where I learned to hate losing.

When I was first called up to varsity, we were playing at Rutherford and were up 6–0. We had a cornerback, two years older than me, who got beat for a touchdown. We lost 7–6.

I sat on the bus with my head down, trying not to make eye contact with anyone. But I looked up when this kid got on the bus, his helmet still strapped up, mouthpiece still in, tears rolling down his face, snot bubbles coming out of his nose. He rode the whole way home like that.

On that bus ride, I made a promise to myself: that would never be me. I was going to work harder than anybody, do whatever I had to do to make sure I was never that kid. Losing wasn't an option.

That Jersey mentality never left me. And it absolutely played a role in how my football career played out.

• • •

The recruiting letters from colleges started coming my sophomore year. My parents loved it; my mother would organize them, sorting every letter I got into alphabetical order. I didn't pay much attention to them until my junior year, when I started to get letters from schools around the country. Texas. USC. Hawaii. I'd get letters for both football and basketball, but I kept waiting for that one offer that would've made up my mind for me. "Florida State? That's cool. But where's the letter from Miami?" That one never came. Neither did the one from Mike Krzyzewski. Those letters would've made up my mind for me.

My mom sat me down one day and asked me what I wanted to do. And I told her the truth—I didn't know. I couldn't make up my mind. Would it be football or basketball?

My AAU coach, Bob Hurley, had suggested to John Calipari that he come visit me. Cal sat in my house and told me that it would be a big mistake if I chose football. As I sat there listening to him tell me what he was building at UMass, I wondered if my destiny was to play basketball.

I took a double visit down to Virginia. I spent time with John Crotty and the basketball team the first day, Chris Slade and the football team the second day. I loved it there. Loved the campus, loved the guys. It was my first recruiting trip, and I was ready to sign right away. But as my father reminded me, "We made other appointments. We have to keep them."

So, I went to Syracuse, got off the plane, and was greeted by what looked like four feet of snow on the ground. I turned to my father and said, "We can get back on the plane and go home right now if you want."

But we stayed, and I got to meet with Dick MacPherson, who had taken Syracuse to four straight bowl games. We went to see a basketball game in the Carrier Dome, and he told me, "You know you can play basketball here, too. We have some guys who do that already."

Then we started talking football. "We're going to redshirt you, but don't worry," he said. "I'm going to be here all five years that you're here. I'm telling you, I am going to be here."

He gave me his whole pitch, and I went home to think about it.

Three days later, he left to become head coach of the Patriots.

After that, I told my parents that I didn't want to take any more recruiting visits. I had made up my mind.

I was going to Rutgers.

My father had told me early on that he didn't care which school I chose. He and my mom would be at every game, he assured me, no matter where it was. It would be my choice. Only one thing was non-negotiable:

"They are going to use you for your talent. You are going to use them to get your education. If you don't graduate…"

He didn't have to finish his sentence. I knew I was dead if I didn't get my degree.

I think they were surprised at first when I chose Rutgers. But I knew it was the right place. I think I had probably decided around Thanksgiving of my junior year.

We were playing North Arlington, and I looked up in the stands and saw Rutgers head coach Doug Graber and his son. They had come to watch me play on Thanksgiving.

After the game, he pulled me aside and said, "Listen, I know you have a lot of stuff going on. And I know you have basketball to consider. But I'm telling you something right now. I'm going to give you a scholarship to play football at Rutgers. Even if you get hurt between now and then and you can't play, I'm giving you that scholarship to Rutgers."

I knew right then I'd met someone who would have my back. Just like I had in Harrison.

I still took my other visits. I still took calls from Lou Holtz at Notre Dame. I still went to camp at Penn State. Joe Paterno came down to the field, put me in the cart with him, and told me, "We're recruiting three quarterbacks. If you say yes right now, I'm dumping the other two."

I was surprised, but I explained to him that I was going into my senior year, and that I couldn't commit right then.

He stopped the cart: "Get out." And that was cool, hearing him say that in that unique voice of his.

Rutgers was the right fit for a lot of reasons. First off, I'd be close to home, which was important to me because I was a big mama's boy. I still am. I've always had a super tight relationship with my mom, my valentine before there were any other valentines. For a long time, she joked that my wife was "the other woman," a joke she kept up until I was in my forties. It would be good to be just a 30-minute drive from home, where I had my family, where I could get my laundry done, where I could eat my mother's lasagna.

And there was another reason. When I made my decision about college, I asked my parents, "Why would a Jersey boy go to Pennsylvania and make their school better?" Penn State and Syracuse and Boston College were always coming in and taking guys out of Jersey. Not me. I'm from Jersey. I was going to Rutgers.

I have to say, however, that my recruiting visit to Rutgers was the worst ever. A receiver named Jimmy Guarantano was my host. Instead of going out to a bar like we did everywhere else, he took me to the movies. With his girlfriend. I'm not even sure he bought me popcorn.

Still, I went to Rutgers. My parents, my sister, Alicen, and my girlfriend got to see me play. They came to all my games, except one—at Cincinnati, November 1992, my redshirt freshman season. We lost that day 26–24, finished the season with a 7–4 record, and didn't get invited to a bowl game. Rutgers hadn't been to a bowl game since 1978, and an eight-win season would have earned us an invitation somewhere. I didn't talk to my dad for two months.

We never did make it to a bowl game during my years at Rutgers. But it absolutely was the right place for me to go.

And five years after he spent his Thanksgiving recruiting me, it was Doug Graber who first suggested to Bill Parcells that he give me a look.

From there, everything I learned in Harrison would have to earn me my shot.

3

Maybe

anging out down at the Annie Bridge, drinking with my teammates, I learned, among other things, how to try to hide the truth from my parents.

I was a freshman and had an 11:00 PM curfew, which meant I would stop drinking at 9:30, then head over to Gina's pizzeria for a couple of slices. I'd put 10 pounds of garlic on my pizza, so much that I could hardly even stand to chew it. It was disgusting. I'd be eating and sweating and crying from the garlic. But I'd finish it off, splash water on my face, and then run home, because some asshole senior told me that if you run, you would sweat all the beer out of your system. It took me about two years to realize that the trick didn't work, that the only thing that came from running a mile home full of beer and pizza and 10 pounds of garlic was I'd get sick to my stomach.

When I got home, I wouldn't even breathe in front of my parents. I'd give them a quick "I'm kinda tired, so I'm just going to go up to bed. Good night." All without ever cracking open my mouth enough to let any air out.

Amazingly, I once tried the same shit with Bill Parcells during my first season in the NFL.

J.R. Conrad was an offensive lineman from Oklahoma who was on the Patriots practice squad with me. We also lived in the same apartment building, so on Friday nights, we'd go out together down in Providence.

One Saturday morning, toward the end of the 1996 season, Conrad and I came into the team meeting smelling like shit. We'd been up all night, drinking gin and 7-Ups. Probably had about 30 of them. And when I got to the meeting room, I passed Parcells and, of course, I tried not to breathe near him. The same sneaky shit I tried to pull on my parents back in Harrison.

He wasn't buying it.

"What the fuck are you doing?"

"Nothing," I answered, trying not to open my mouth.

"What, do you go out every fucking night here? Going out to Providence all the time? You think I don't know where my players are?"

I couldn't figure out how he'd found out, and I started to explain that, well, it was a Friday night, and that we only had walkthroughs on Saturday. Then he cut me off.

"You know what? Shut the fuck up."

After a few seconds of silence, he continued.

"We're going to bring you up. I'm putting you on the active roster."

I had no idea how to react.

My first thought was to jump up and hug him. Instead, I just froze.

"Are you all right?"

All I could get out was, "Yeah."

He told me to go see his secretary and sign the contract. They were going to pay me the league minimum, which if I recall correctly was around $98,000 at the time. Which was fine with me.

The next thing I needed to do was call Cecy.

I first met Cecy Matias when I was in eighth grade. She was a junior in high school, taller than me, and didn't have a lot of interest in this crazy, annoying little kid with braces and an Afro.

That didn't stop me from dogging her everywhere. I would knock her books down, go ring her doorbell and leave a cassette tape of love songs for her to listen to. You know, totally smooth.

One day, my best friend, Mike, and I were riding our bikes around town, and we saw Cecy and her best friend. It was time to make my move.

We followed them for a while until Cecy turned to me and asked, "What do I have to do for you to go away and leave us alone?"

"All you gotta do is kiss me."

"That's it?"

She laughed but, by some miracle, she agreed. So, I got off my bike, went up to her—had to stretch my neck so I could reach her—and we kissed. And Mike kissed Cecy's friend. One die, all die.

Then, as we promised, we got on our bikes and rode away. Mike was out of his mind. He couldn't believe what just happened.

On that ride back to my house, I told him, "I am gonna marry that girl someday."

When I got the good news from Parcells, Cecy and I still hadn't gotten married. But we'd been together pretty much from that first kiss. We dated through high school and college, even though she took some ribbing from people because I was only a freshman when she was a senior. She had already started working when I was at Rutgers and she would buy me things when I had no money of my own. She bought a car and let me drive it to school; she took the train into New York City. Sometimes, I would pick her up at the train station, and she'd have a new pair of sneakers for me. I would always promise her, "Someday, baby." Someday, I would take care of her the way she deserved to be taken care of.

But even when I got to the NFL and was on the practice squad, she was still making more money at her job in the city than I was. Still, I would send money home to her in Harrison, just like the veterans on the team told me I should. William Roberts and Pepper Johnson tried to teach me about the importance of saving money.

"Every time you get paid, buy yourself something you need: jeans, a shirt. Not jewelry, not a gold watch, not a car," they told me. "Pay what you need to pay, then put the rest of it away."

Finally, I was able to contribute and help pay the rent for the apartment Cecy and our 18-month-old daughter, Rayven, were living in behind Cecy's aunt's house. When I got called up to the active roster, the first thing I did was call my girls back home and tell them I'd made the team.

And what a great team it was to be part of. We had started the season 0–2, but we won 11 of our last 14 and wound up the No. 2 seed in the AFC playoffs. Our team was loaded. We had Drew Bledsoe and Curtis Martin. Vincent Brisby and Troy Brown. Roberts and Bruce Armstrong and Ben Coates. On defense, we had Ted Johnson and Chris Slade, Willie McGinest and Ty Law.

Even the rookie class was solid. There was Terry Glenn and Tedy Bruschi. And, of course, Lawyer Milloy, who was an absolute beast.

Then there was Parcells' staff. Ray Perkins was the offensive coordinator. We had Chris Palmer and Maurice Carthon and Charlie Weis. Al Groh was the defensive coordinator. Romeo Crennel coached the defensive line and Dante Scarnecchia coached the linebackers. And the secondary coach, who was also our assistant head coach, was Bill Belichick.

I hadn't added much in my two games playing special teams. I might never have gotten a chance to do anything else if it hadn't been for Kordell Stewart.

Mike Tomczak was the starting quarterback for the Pittsburgh Steelers that season. He had replaced Neil O'Donnell, who left for the Jets as a free agent after leading the Steelers to Super Bowl XXX.

But Pittsburgh had found a weapon on its roster that nobody could stop.

Kordell had been a quarterback in college, and he had a cannon—anyone who remembers his Hail Mary to Michael Westbrook that helped Colorado upset Michigan knows what kind of arm he had. To make it in the NFL, he was willing to do whatever Steelers head coach Bill Cowher asked him to do.

He played wide receiver. He ran the ball. He threw the ball. He was a receiver/running back/quarterback—hence the nickname Slash. And in 1996, Slash was becoming a problem for defensive coordinators.

In the Steelers' playoff opener, Kordell scored on a one-yard run in the first quarter, completed a pass on a two-point conversion in the third quarter, then rushed for another short touchdown in the fourth quarter. Pittsburgh beat Indianapolis 42–14, and was now coming to Foxborough to play us. It was the first home playoff game for the Patriots since the team lost to Earl Campbell, Dan Pastorini, and the Oilers in 1978.

On Wednesday morning, after all the coaches had met and put together the game plan for Pittsburgh, Bill Parcells said to me those magic words every player wants to hear:

"We need you."

At that point, I was playing on special teams and running wide receiver on the scout team. Now, Bill Belichick needed me to take some snaps at quarterback so our defense could get ready for Slash.

"We need you," Parcells told me. "We need you to play quarterback, go out there and use your legs, run around and stuff."

I said, "Okay," but fireworks were going off inside my head. What I really was thinking was, *Big mistake, Coach. BIG. You are asking for trouble now.*

I already took scout team seriously. It was our job to get the defense ready, to give them good looks at what they could expect from a receiver they were about to line up against.

This was different. Now, I was getting to do my thing. I knew what I had to do.

That first day at practice, I killed it. I was running and making throws all over the place. Belichick was getting pretty pissed at his guys, and those guys were getting pissed at me. I hadn't taken a snap at quarterback since my last game at Rutgers, but I still kicked their ass so bad, Belichick made them come in the next morning at 6:30.

On Thursday, I did the same thing. Then Willie McGinest got me.

I was on the move, out of the pocket, made the throw, and Willie just decleated me. In practice, the regular quarterbacks have the red jerseys on. Not on scout team. They can hit you on scout team. And he nailed me.

I jumped right up and started going after him. Willie just laughed a little and said, "This kid's crazy."

Before I could say anything, Parcells weighed in.

"No, he's not. He's fuckin' Jersey."

Shortly after that, Belichick told me to stay in the pocket, but I'd already accomplished my mission: I got our defense ready. Kordell Stewart went 0-for-10 against us, rushed for 19 yards, didn't catch a pass, didn't score a touchdown. And I thought maybe I'd opened some eyes in my one chance to play quarterback.

As it turned out, it wasn't my only chance.

The next week, we had Jacksonville coming to town for the AFC Championship Game. And that meant Mark Brunell. Brunell was on his way to becoming a Pro Bowl quarterback. In 1996, he passed for 4,300 yards, ran for 400 more, and had a second-year franchise one win away from the Super Bowl.

Again, Parcells and Belichick needed me out there on scout team, playing the part of the scrambling left-handed quarterback. And, again, I was killing people out there. I was pump-faking, running past them, jumping and throwing the ball when I was in the air. I was even better as Brunell than I was as Kordell.

At the end of that Thursday practice, I crossed paths with Parcells coming off the field. As we passed each other, he said, "I don't know, kid. Maybe."

As in, "Maybe you can be a quarterback."

For me, it was like the heavens opened up.

"Maybe."

It was all the air I needed to breathe at that moment.

Talk about catching a break. If we were playing Dan Marino or pretty much any other quarterback in the league, someone else would have run scout team quarterback. I would have never been able to show Parcells and the other coaches my skills in a live situation. Kordell Stewart and Mark Brunell were pretty much the only two guys I resembled at that time, and we played them both in the playoffs, in consecutive weeks. Amazing.

Even better, we destroyed Jacksonville 20–6. Brunell had his worst day of the season. And the New England Patriots were going to Super Bowl XXXI, down in New Orleans. Which meant that I was going to the Super Bowl. Me. I didn't go to a single bowl game at Rutgers. Now, I was going to the biggest fucking game on the planet.

My girls came, my parents came, my sister, my boys from Harrison. I probably had 30 people I needed to find tickets for.

Ironically, we were playing Green Bay—the same team we faced in our first preseason game that year. They had Brett Favre and Reggie White and LeRoy Butler. It was the second of Favre's three straight MVP seasons. But we didn't give a fuck.

I was standing in the tunnel, ready to run out into the Superdome on Super Bowl Sunday. I was on both kickoff units, so it didn't matter if we were kicking or receiving—I was going to be on the field for the first play of the Super Bowl. There was so much emotion running through me. I was crying and angry and happy, all at the same time. I really wasn't sure what to feel.

All of a sudden, *boom!* Someone punched me dead in my chest. It took me totally by surprise, and it damn near knocked the wind out of me.

And there was Parcells, right in my face.

"Didn't I tell you I was gonna take you here?"

I lost my mind. Here we were, in the tunnel, the guy who gave me my shot, the guy who put me on the team. The guy who told me to trust him, that he'd figure out what to do with me. The guy who finally had given me a chance to play quarterback, and who thought maybe there was something there.

Parcells. The Lombardi Trophy, right there in front of us. The crowd. I could have run through a wall right then. I nearly bit right through my mouthpiece. I had to go hit something. I was going to burst.

We were up 14–10 in the second quarter when Green Bay scored to take the lead. I remember seeing Lawyer Milloy getting caught on Antonio Freeman, and Favre knew he had us. They had a receiver on the outside who motioned inside, and Ty Law was supposed to kick him over to Milloy. But he didn't move. And Milloy got stuck on Freeman. As soon as they snapped the ball, we were on the sideline saying, "Oh, shit." Favre hit Freeman down the right sideline, and he went

81 yards for a touchdown. The longest touchdown pass in Super Bowl history at that point.

At halftime, we were down 27–14. Everyone in our locker room was pissed. Max Lane was getting the shit kicked out of him by Reggie White, who smashed him with one of his club moves. I'd never seen a lineman that big flying through the air like that. Bruce Armstrong lost his shit, yelling that he was going to gut someone.

Late in the third quarter, we cut the lead to 27–21. Curtis Martin scored on an 18-yard run, and it was now a one-possession game. We'd stopped Green Bay twice in that third quarter, and we were all fired up when I went out onto the field for the kickoff.

I was lined up at R2, second player from the right. Inside of me was Larry Whigham, a Pro Bowl special teams player. We were running down the field, neck-and-neck. At one point, I looked to my left and I saw Larry's feet in the air, up by my shoulders. He'd been completely taken out by a Green Bay blocker.

Desmond Howard fielded the ball at the 1-yard line and started straight upfield. I got inside my man and started to come at him from behind. I was at full speed, about five yards away, and I thought I had him. I figured I'd just pump my arms twice more, dive at his feet, and he'd be mine.

I pumped my arms twice, looked up, and…nothing. Motherfucker's 12 yards ahead of me already. And there was no way I was going to catch him.

I started doing that kind of exaggerated running that looks like you're running as hard as you can but you're really not. I wasn't going to get him, but it looks good on film. Desmond

Howard scored—a 99-yard touchdown, the longest play in Super Bowl history at the time.

I went over to the sideline while Green Bay went for the two-point conversion, which they got. Favre to Mark Chmura. I had learned already not to come to the sideline near Parcells. Sneak in wherever you can, just don't let him see you. Parcells came storming down the sideline, furious, wanting to know who blew their assignment on Howard's return.

"Who the hell was it?"

I didn't say anything. After the conversion, I ran straight back out to the field for the kickoff return. And when I got back to the sideline, there he was again, trying to find out who'd blown his assignment.

"Lucas, get the fuck over here. Who was it? Was it you?"

"It wasn't me, Coach."

"Who was it?"

"I don't know."

"Are you gonna tell me who it was?"

I wasn't going to rat out a teammate. I wasn't going to tell Parcells anything. Not right then.

"I don't know."

"Get out of my sight."

Which was what I was trying to do from the beginning.

No one scored after that. We lost 35–21. Desmond Howard was named the Super Bowl MVP. Brett Favre ran around like an asshole with his helmet off.

We went into the locker room and sat there, one last time, as a team.

Parcells came in.

"I like some of you," he said. "I really like a lot of you. I don't like some of you. We had a good run."

And then he was out the door.

I looked around, wondering what just happened. "Wasn't he supposed to say something more?"

We flew home the next day. He wasn't even on the plane. That was it. That's how he left. That was the end.

Within a couple of months, Parcells was gone. He had moved on to become head coach of the New York Jets.

Belichick was gone. Charlie Weis, Maurice Carthon, Romeo Crennel, Al Groh, all gone.

I wound up with an AFC championship ring that I didn't want and never wore. I tried to give it to my father years later, but he didn't want it either. Who wanted to be reminded of losing the Super Bowl?

Bill Parcells always said, "You are what your record says you are."

We had lost. And no one remembers the losers.

4

"I Just Don't Think You're Good Enough"

By the time the next training camp rolled around, everything had changed.

For starters, I was a married man.

Over the winter, I had taken Cecy to see her favorite Broadway show, *Phantom of the Opera*. She loves the scene where the guy is singing to the girl on the rooftops. And the song, "All I Ask of You" is Cecy's favorite; she cries every time she hears it.

We were watching the show, and when they got to that scene, I elbowed her to get her attention. She was probably pissed that I'd interrupted her favorite song, but when she turned, I had taken out the box with the engagement ring and opened it.

In the middle of the song, Cecy screamed "Oh my god!" I'm sure the lady on the stage heard her. I know the woman in front of us did; she turned around and gave us a nasty look and shushed us.

When Cecy screamed, I panicked. I snapped the box closed and put it right back in my pocket. At intermission, we went out to the lobby and got some champagne and I gave her the ring.

In June 1997, we got married.

Soon after I went back up to New England for the start of training camp, Cecy quit her job in the city, packed up everything in Harrison, and she and Rayven moved up to Massachusetts.

I was a little nervous about her coming. I wasn't sure what would happen now that Parcells was gone. I had to prove myself all over again to a new coaching staff, and I wasn't sure what they thought of me or whether I was even going to make the roster. The thought of her giving up her salary and her insurance worried me.

Still, Cecy wanted to be part of what I was going through. A lot of players had their wives and kids around all the time, and she wanted to be there to share the experience with me. For as long as it would last.

So, we moved into a two-bedroom, two-bathroom apartment in North Attleboro, which was great. In Harrison, we had nothing. We had one bedroom, one bathroom, and there were always skunks outside. Now, we had two bathrooms. And carpet. That was a big deal for us.

Pete Carroll was the new Patriots coach. He had been the head coach of the Jets for one season, and was coming to New England after two seasons as the defensive coordinator in San Francisco.

I couldn't get a read on what he thought of me. He knew me as a special teams guy. That's really what I was then—a very good special teams guy. He hadn't seen those practices when I played quarterback and tore up our defense.

In our first preseason game (again, against Green Bay), I made a couple of tackles on special teams. Nothing special, nothing to give me an indication one way or the other how things would go down.

The next game, I didn't play. Zero snaps.

I went to Pete and asked, "Is there a problem here?" He didn't say much, but it became pretty clear what he thought of me when I didn't get on the field in the third preseason game.

That was a Sunday.

On Tuesday, Bobby Grier, who had been promoted to vice president of player personnel after Parcells left and was a great guy, found me in the building.

"Pete wants to see you, Ray. I'm sorry."

I went into Carroll's office, pissed off already. He had never really given me a shot, and now he was going to cut me. Two weeks after my wife and baby had moved up from Harrison.

He was just sitting there when I walked in, behind his big desk like the Godfather. There weren't any lights on in the room. Before I could sit down, he cut me.

"I just don't think you're good enough to play in the NFL. I'm sorry."

He put his hand out, and it took all the restraint I had not to smack it away.

"Hey, Pete," I said. (I never called Coach Parcells by his first name.) "You haven't heard the last of me."

With that, I bounced straight out of the room.

And straight into the unknown.

I was livid by the time I got back to the apartment. I had a bottle of Jack Daniel's with me, so Cecy knew right away this was not going to be good. I had no one else to take it out on, so I started fighting with her.

"I told you not to quit your job. We have no money coming in. What the fuck are we gonna do now?"

I had no idea. Neither did she. Should we stay there, with the two bathrooms and the carpet? Move back to Harrison? We went to bed that night with no jobs and no answers.

At 6:00 AM the following morning, the phone rang and woke us up.

"Who the fuck is this?" I yelled.

I didn't really care who it was. I was still in a pretty dark mood, and whoever was on the other end was going to get a taste.

"What the fuck is going on up there?"

It was Parcells.

I sat up immediately and told him what had happened.

"He never gave me a shot, Coach."

"He didn't, huh?"

"No. He didn't."

"All right," he said. "Get your ass to Providence in the next hour. There's a plane ticket waiting for you. If you miss this flight, don't bother coming."

There was no way in hell I was going to miss that flight.

I turned to Cecy: "Baby, I gotta go. Like, right this second."

It was insane. We shoved a couple of things into a bag, grabbed the baby, and jumped in the car. I was cruising, driving on the shoulder, doing whatever I had to do to make that flight.

I landed at LaGuardia Airport and caught a ride to the Jets practice facility. The bus was already there, and guys were loading onto it. We were leaving pretty much immediately to fly to Tampa for the final preseason game. Everyone boarding the bus was in jackets and slacks; I was in shorts and a T-shirt. It was all I had time to pack.

Parcells saw me right away. Before I could say anything, he said, "Get on the fucking bus."

Just like that, I was back in the game. I was the newest member of the New York Jets.

That night, we had our meetings in the hotel. They already had me penciled in to be on all the special teams units against the Bucs.

I did not play well in that game. I was blocking for Dedric Ward on one kickoff return, missed an assignment, and nearly got him killed. Dedric came up to me on the sideline and started yelling at me.

"What are you doing out there?"

To be honest, I had no idea what I was doing.

"Dude, I just got here, and I don't even know what fucking scheme we're running."

Final cuts were coming after that game. And I knew there was at least one person who didn't want me around.

Bill Belichick didn't really like me as a player. But you don't overrule Parcells, and he wanted me there. So, again, I started the season on the practice squad. And I stayed there for three months.

The day before we were scheduled to play the Vikings in Week 13, I was brought up to the active roster to play special teams. We were 7–4 and making a push for the playoffs. Which was amazing, considering the Jets had gone 1–15 under Rich Kotite the year before.

In the middle of the game, without any warning or preparation, Parcells called my number.

"Ray, get behind center."

Out came Neil O'Donnell, and into the game, to play quarterback in the National Football League, was me. Special teams guy. From Harrison. Not-good-enough-for-the-Patriots Ray Lucas.

The call was for me to run a quarterback draw. The play had been in the game plan, but we'd never really worked on it. I knew what I had to do.

I took the snap, dropped back two steps, and I took off like a bat out of hell. I hit the hole and ran for my life down the middle of the field. Fifteen-yard gain. First down.

And out I came.

I got to the sideline where Parcells grabbed me.

"You know, I think you could play some quarterback here. I really do."

My days of impersonating a wide receiver were finished. From that day forward, I was an NFL quarterback. An NFL quarterback who played on special teams, of course, which made me pretty unique. They only gave me three plays to run—the quarterback draw, a dive option, and a sprint pass. But I was a quarterback. Even if they still hadn't listed me as one on the roster for the next game up in Buffalo.

I didn't take a snap against the Bills or in the game after.

But in Week 16, I ran two quarterback draws for 10 yards in a 31–0 win over Tampa Bay. We were 9–6 with a shot at a wild card berth, heading into our last game of the season at Detroit.

It turned out to be an unforgettable contest, for a lot of reasons.

It was the game during which Barry Sanders broke the 2,000-yard mark.

It was the first game during which I saw more than one snap at quarterback. I'd gone in to run the draw, and after the play, I started heading to the sideline, as usual. But then I saw something that surprised me—Parcells was waving his arms, telling me to stay on the field.

We were up 10–6 in the third quarter. And Parcells had me out there. Not O'Donnell. Not Chuck Clements or Glenn Foley, the other two quarterbacks listed on the roster.

I ran a couple of rollouts. I completed the first three passes of my career. And then I threw an interception from Detroit's 29-yard line. Another career first.

It also happened to be the game during which linebacker Reggie Brown was nearly paralyzed tackling Adrian Murrell. I didn't see the hit when it happened, but I saw him turn from blue to purple on the field. We all took a knee, and I saw the doctors giving him mouth-to-mouth. The game was stopped for 17 minutes before they got Reggie, unconscious and motionless, into an ambulance. He wound up with a bruised spinal cord, and, thanks only to a surgery that fused a couple of vertebrae in his neck, he was able to walk again. But his football career, just two seasons old, was over.

When you see something like that happen, you pray that the guy's going to be okay. It doesn't matter which side of the ball he's on or even which team he's on. But then you have to treat it like you do every other injury. You have to let it go. You have to go back out there. And you can't be thinking about the violence of the game or you will get yourself killed.

We went out there after the injury to Reggie Brown, down 13–10 after Sanders scored early in the fourth quarter. We moved the ball down to the 9-yard line, and then Leon Johnson threw an interception on a halfback option pass intended for Jeff Graham.

Game over. Season over.

But for me, the next chapter of my career had only just begun. To get ready for it, I needed to make a decision.

Which one of my knees would I get surgically repaired in the off-season? Because they both needed to be fixed.

I hadn't injured either of them on any specific play. It was just that the natural wear and tear of two NFL seasons—on scout team, on special teams, running my three-play repertoire at quarterback—and everything that had come before had taken their toll.

There were nights when I couldn't go upstairs to my bedroom; the stairs were too steep for my knees to handle it. Coming down was worse. Sometimes, I would be walking downstairs feeling like my whole knee was about to blow apart.

There were days I couldn't work the gas pedal without pain. Days I couldn't swing my legs out of the car. The pain would be so severe down the front of my leg, it would feel like there was nothing connected inside my knee.

I would will myself through practice. Once you're out there and you start practicing, you get lathered up and the adrenaline starts flowing, the pain starts to subside a little bit. Besides, you have no time to worry about it. You've got your job to do.

But when you get back to the locker room after practice, or when you have to go lift weights, or when you have to go upstairs to watch film, that's when the pain bites back. That's when you go to the training room for ice treatment.

I hated the ice treatments, especially the ice bath. It was like a full-body brain freeze. But you had to do it—especially after one of those Parcells three-a-days—or you'd fall apart.

The water in the ice bath was about 40 degrees. If you went into 40-degree water outside in the wintertime, before too long, you'd be dead. We actually had to put booties on our toes before we went in the tub or they'd get frostbite. I'd get in and the pain was damn near unbearable. For two minutes and 32 seconds. Believe me, I know that for a fact. I used to time myself to see how long it would take to get numb. I'd go numb and stay in the tub for 30 minutes in 40-degree water up to my waist. Some guys were so crazy, they'd go underwater up to their shoulders. Usually the wide receivers.

When you got out of the tub, you couldn't really walk. Every muscle was clenched. But then that would wear off, and it was like you had been dipped in the Fountain of Youth. The pain had melted away.

Even when I wasn't in the tub, I still needed the ice. I'm not talking about a little ice pack, either. I'm talking two big plastic bags, seven pounds apiece, for each leg. I'd put one on the front and one on the back so that my entire knee was encased in ice, and wrap enough plastic wrap around it to hold 14 pounds of ice in place. And then I'd be off, walking like Frankenstein, to go watch film or cutups for 90 minutes.

At some point, I would be done with the ice and remove the bags. Now, I was ready to walk back downstairs, but I couldn't feel anything in my legs or feet. They'd still be totally numb. So, I held the railing on my way down the stairs, walking like a geriatric, one step at a time.

Then, I'd go get my anti-inflammatories, the Motrin or whatever they were giving out at the time. And I'd grab some Ambien to help me sleep at night.

By the time I got out to my car, the numbness had worn off. I'd start driving, start getting stiff, and when I moved my foot or ankle even slightly, it felt like someone was grinding a gear shift in my knee again. I had pain like that so often, I learned to drive with two feet.

My legs were what made me different as a quarterback, and I needed to get them right if I was going to have a chance to get on the field under center in 1998.

The doctors gave me a choice to do one knee or the other. I chose to do both of them at the same time.

I decided it would be best to have the less-invasive arthroscopic surgery on my right knee and the full-blown surgery on my left. My reasoning? My right leg was my pivot leg. The one I transferred all my weight to before I made a throw. If I were to open that one up, it might take longer to heal than it would from getting scoped. And I didn't have that kind of time. I needed to get back to the practice field and the weight room so I could keep my job.

For a right-handed quarterback, the left leg is just a stopper. So, I had them cut that knee and scope the right, even though the right turned out to be in far worse shape. Right after the season ended, they went into my left knee, reattached the patella tendon, and at the same time, scoped my right knee and cleaned it up as best they could.

Then came the rehab, which put me in the hands of Dave Price, the head athletic trainer for the Jets, who was by far the best trainer I ever worked with. He actually was an honest human being in a job where you don't find too many honest human beings. Dave Price genuinely cared about his players. I used to see him rubbing Curtis Martin's feet; where in his contract does it say he has to do that? Not all trainers truly care. At least not the way Dave does.

Trainers in the NFL are in a tricky position. Their job is to take care of the players, but it's also their job to get the players back out on the field. That comes straight from the top: "Get him out of the training room, I don't care what you have to do." If guys don't get back out there fast enough, trainers lose their jobs.

Parcells didn't want players just hanging around in the training room, so he'd made sure Dave kept the training room at about 50 degrees. No way you were getting comfortable in there.

Also, Dave had the TV tuned in to NASCAR all the time. I'd always ask him if we could change the channel, and his answer was always the same: "Absolutely not." I still have no idea whether Dave really was a NASCAR fan or if Parcells had instructed him to keep it on that channel. No one was going to be hanging out in Antarctica watching NASCAR any longer than they had to.

Throughout my rehab, Dave was great. He never asked, "Is that enough?" It was, "How much more do you want to do?" He pushed me the way I wanted to be pushed, the way I needed to be pushed so I wouldn't miss any of the off-season program. I couldn't miss minicamp. Three plays on a resume does not a quarterback make, and I knew that if I missed any practice time, I was going to be home next fall watching football from my couch.

I was lucky that one of my best friends on the team, Richie Anderson, was going through rehab at the same time. Richie's patella tendon had worn down so much, he was thinking it could snap at any second, on any step he took, any play we ran. We had surgery at the same time and were going through rehab at the same time. That gave me more than a partner to work out with; it gave me someone to compete against.

You have to understand that professional athletes compete *everywhere*. It's not just during the games. It's on the practice field, where they're fighting for their jobs, fighting for reps. It's in the weight room. That motor never shuts off. Someone pulls up next to me at a traffic light, I'm going first when it turns green. I'm flooring it.

The NFL didn't make us into this kind of person. We made it into the NFL because we were like this already.

It's not something we realize we're doing. It's not a decision we make about how we want to be. It's in us. It's not something you can learn; it is always there. And it's not something you have to think about. You just do it.

As crazy as it may sound, we competed just as hard in the training room as we did on the practice field. Losing sucks, wherever you're doing it.

Richie and I would be in the training room, trying to outdo each other. "I can bend my knee farther back than you can." "How much weight are you able to do today?"

We'd both be hooked up to the electrical stimulation machine, which basically shoots currents into your body to activate the nerves. Richie and I competed to see who could take more stim. "Look! I'm doing 50. What are you up to?" Our legs would be shaking like we'd just been Tasered, but we'd crank up the machine a notch higher. "I'm at 51! Do 51!"

That is the mentality of a football player. We are willing to literally hurt ourselves while we're trying to get better.

We'd be in the weight room, and the strength coach would tell us not to go down past 90 degrees when we were squatting. He'd give us our regimen but wouldn't be watching over us. As soon as he was out of sight, we'd squat past 90 degrees.

Sometimes, Richie and I would get massages. An acupuncturist would come in and then rub down our legs. We would compete over how many needles we could take. "I'm at 150? Can you do 150?" And who could take them in the strangest places.

We would compete to see who could put the biggest dip of chewing tobacco in our mouths. The competition never ended. Ever.

One morning before practice, Leon Johnson showed up in the locker room with a mayonnaise jar filled with some nasty moonshine his uncle had made back in North Carolina. It smelled so bad, none of us could imagine anyone drinking this shit. Which pretty much meant the competition was on.

I said I could take a sip. The instant this stuff touched my lips, it felt like someone had lit a fire in my esophagus.

Glenn Foley stepped up. "That's it? I'll drink it." He took a gulp of it; an hour later, he was asleep in the meeting room.

This is who we are. We are creatures of competition. It's part drive-to-be-the-best, part survival instinct.

With my knee surgeries and rehab behind me, my body was ready for another season of fighting for my professional life.

5

Squatting Seven Plates

lenn Foley and I were walking through the equipment room one morning during the summer of 1998, on our way to the dining hall in the Jets facility at Hofstra University. Foley, who had started a couple of games in place of Neil O'Donnell the season before, was going to be the starter in 1998. I was fighting to be his backup.

A bunch of guys were lifting as usual, but we saw something that made us stop.

We noticed a guy standing under a bar that looked like a rainbow—bent with seven 45-pound plates on both sides. He was squatting about 650 pounds.

It wasn't Jumbo Elliott or Matt O'Dwyer or one of the other guys on the offensive line you'd expect to see throwing up that kind of weight. Instead, it was some dude I didn't recognize, his hair standing up all over the place, wearing a big leather weightlifter's belt that the strength coach was straining to make as tight as it could be.

We watched as the guy underneath all that weight went down, came up, and racked it. It was incredible. I wondered who it was, so I asked Foley if he'd seen the guy before.

"Oh, that's Vinny Testaverde. He just signed."

My reaction was immediate: "Oh fuck. That's it for me. How am I supposed to compete with that?"

That off-season, the Jets had loaded up. First, we brought in Kevin Mawae, who would become an All-Pro center and a fixture on the Jets offensive line for eight years. Then, we signed Curtis Martin, a restricted free agent, away from New England. He was already a Pro Bowl running back on his way to the Hall of Fame, and the Jets paid a bundle—a big contract for Curtis, plus draft picks to the Patriots as compensation—to bring him in. Later in the summer, we'd sign Bryan Cox.

In June, just before the start of training camp, the Jets signed Vinny and let O'Donnell walk. The original plan was that Vinny—a Heisman Trophy winner, the first pick in the 1987 draft, and an 11-year vet with a 4,000-yard season and a trip to the Pro Bowl on his résumé—would back up Foley, and that I would be the third quarterback and keep going balls to the wall on special teams.

That was the plan...until we lost the first two games Foley started. Vinny started the next two, and we won both. By Game 6, Vinny had become the full-time starter. We won 10 of our last 11 games, won the AFC East for the first time in Jets history, and made the playoffs for the first time since 1991.

I didn't get much time at quarterback that year. I still had my three plays in the game plan—even if I never got any reps in practice—but I only threw three passes that year, only ran the ball five times.

Still, it was maybe the best year of my career. And a lot of that had to do with Vinny.

While I was rehabbing my knee, I was focused on one thing—doing everything I had to do to get back on the field. Every time I worked out, I would ask myself afterward, "Did I do enough? Did I put in enough time? Should I have kept going?" I never wanted to say down the road someday, "If only I had done more."

Vinny Testaverde lived his entire life that way.

When he was a junior in high school, Vinny had gone with his football coaches to a camp that was modeled after an NFL training camp. It was pretty hard-core in its approach to training and running. He got paired up with a senior running back who was in great shape and was devoted to working and practicing hard. That guy became Vinny's role model.

Years later, Vinny became mine.

When I saw a horse like Vinny squatting seven plates, I'd think, *Well, then I have to squat seven plates, too.* It's the nature of competition. I couldn't allow him to be stronger than I was.

Not that he felt much competition from me. Not as a quarterback. I wasn't a threat to his playing time, especially not the way he played in 1998.

Still, he would bust my chops in the weight room to get me going: "Is that all you're doing? I'm an old man and my arms are bigger than yours. You're gonna let an old man outlift you?"

Whatever Vinny could do, I wanted to do. I *had* to do. He helped create the monster.

We lifted together all the time. Two days a week, we'd do chest, shoulders, and triceps; the other days, we'd do legs, back, and biceps. We were squatting 700 pounds, hang cleaning 400 pounds, benching 300 pounds.

The Jets had brought in new equipment when Parcells arrived. But Vinny didn't need a state-of-the-art circuit to work out. He would say, "It's not the arrow. It's the Indian." You can get a great workout with a soup can if you know how to do the right things with it.

I had always been naturally strong. Now, I was learning how to get stronger the right way.

I started eating right. Until I met Vinny, I had never even thought about nutrition. Here was a guy who always watched what he put into his body. "Everything that goes in has to be for a reason," he told me. You can't go around eating Popeye's chicken every day. Your body needs the right fuel the way your mind needs the right fuel. When you eat right, your muscles bounce back from a workout more quickly. You can see the changes in your body. You can see your stomach get cut up.

Vinny made taking care of his body a priority. When he was at the University of Miami, his teammates would go out all the time, even on Friday nights before games. Vinny would rather get a good night's sleep, wake up, and have a great breakfast and a great workout. The guy wound up playing 21 years in the NFL, and was fairly healthy for most of those. Clearly he was on to something.

He wasn't the only one. Curtis Martin would always stay after practice and do extra running. He'd do these 360s, which were basically laps of the perimeter of the football field. You'd start in one corner of an end zone and jog along the end line, which is about 53 yards. Then, you'd turn and sprint the full length of the field, 120 yards. Turn, jog the end line, and then sprint down to the corner where you'd started. About 346 yards in total. And you'd do that four times without stopping. As fast as you could.

At first, I thought he was nuts. Then I figured, if he's doing it, I need to be doing it, too.

Every time I stayed after practice to run with him, I'd be flat on my back afterward, seeing stars or throwing up. I asked him once, "Why do you do all this?"

He said, "Your body tries to limit you. You have to train your mind to tell your body, 'No, I have more.'"

That stuck in my head. My mind wasn't going to let my body limit what I could do. If my shoulder hurt, my mind had to overrule it. Knees acting up? Ignore them. *It doesn't hurt that much. We're gonna keep going.* You have to push past it. Or the game will spit you out.

As Vinny said, "You have to be willing to give your life for the game of football."

I was willing to do just that. I had no choice.

Soon enough, I was in the best shape in my life. I was up to 225 pounds, with about 6 percent body fat. At one point, Parcells told me I was too big, that I had to lose five pounds. We had running backs who were smaller than I was.

Vinny was even more of an influence on me when it came to film study. If Vinny was going in to watch film, I was going in to watch film, too. I needed to know how to see what he saw.

On Mondays, we would get a list of the 150 or so plays the coaches were looking at for the next game. It was always a long list, and quarterbacks needed to start studying those plays right away because we needed to know everything by heart by Wednesday. You had to be able to say, "I see what they're doing on defense. Here's the play. And this is the formation we're running it out of."

That was the hardest part of learning to play quarterback at the NFL level. Every week, we'd get another 150 plays. Most of the time, they'd be the same concepts, but they'd have different names, or we'd run them out of different formations. You'd have one play, but we could run it with four wide receivers or with two tight ends and two backs. We could run the same play out of one formation and then use all kinds of motions and shifts to get guys to different places on the field. You could run the same play 20 different ways, depending on what the matchups tell you in a given week.

On Tuesdays—which are supposed to be an off-day in the NFL—I would go in for whatever treatment I needed, bring my tip sheet with me, and study in the training room. Then, maybe we'd go meet with our quarterbacks coach, Dan Henning. And then Vinny and I would hit the film room together.

Vinny would be watching, say, the Dolphins, looking for tendencies, searching for matchups he could exploit. We'd get a cutup of Sam Madison's plays, see what he did in Cover 3, see what he did in Cover 1. We were watching for anything that could help in a pre-snap read.

And when we found something, we called it out.

"There he goes. He's cheating again with his left leg up and his right one back. He's playing zone."

We would watch film of every down and distance situation that we could possibly face in a game. We'd get a reel of what an opponent did on 3rd and 12, and we'd go through each play.

Then we'd talk through how our plays might match up against that defense. Say we're running Split Right Zoom 574, which might mean Keshawn Johnson runs a curl, Wayne Chrebet runs a corner, and Fred Baxter runs a dig. Then, we'd talk through how that would be defended based on the defense's tendencies.

Essentially, we would be trying to figure out where, against a certain defense, we should go with the ball.

Playing quarterback is all about preparation. And Vinny taught me how to prepare.

He didn't have to do that for me. Not all starting quarterbacks do that. You hear stories about how Brett Favre treated Aaron Rodgers after Green Bay drafted Rodgers out of California. Starting quarterbacks have enough to worry about without helping that guy from special teams.

But Vinny did. He taught me how to eat, taught me how to lift, taught me how to read defenses. He taught me all the important things I needed to know to have a chance to succeed as a quarterback in the NFL.

And he always tried to get me a few snaps. He knew what it was like to have to wait your turn; he sat for two years in college behind Bernie Kosar, thinking he might never get the opportunity to play. But he kept himself ready, just in case the chance came.

So did I. In the locker room before every game, I'd ask Vinny, "You gonna get me in the game today?"

He'd promise he would go out and kick the other team's ass and be up by 30 in the fourth quarter. "Yeah, I'll get you in the game today."

That didn't happen much in 1998. But it was such an important year to me, to my development as a quarterback.

And, of course, we wound up in the AFC Championship Game.

We were beating the Broncos in Denver. It was only 3–0 at halftime but we all knew what was happening. We had it.

We were in total control. This was our game. Everything in my body was telling me that I was going back to the Super Bowl. That the New York Jets were going to the Super Bowl.

Parcells came into the locker room, talked about a few adjustments we needed to make, reminded us to take care of the football, and that was it.

We went out for the second half, Blake Spence blocked a punt, Curtis Martin scored, and we were up 10–0. In John Elway's last home game. Mile High Stadium was stunned silent. It was over.

Then it wasn't.

The play that turned it was a 47-yard completion from Elway to Ed McCaffrey. The wind was blowing right in Elway's face, and he threw a pass that moved like a hot knife through butter. It was a rope; I don't think it ever went higher than eight feet off the ground. The ball was spiraling so tightly, I could read the lettering on the football. It was a one-in-a-million throw.

And we all felt it. *Oh shit. Here it comes.*

Denver scored 23 straight points, we turned the ball over six times over the course of the game, and Elway went back to the Super Bowl.

We went home and immediately turned our attention to getting the job done next season. We were committed to doing everything it took to make 1999 our year.

The first thing I noticed was that I could breathe. Slow, shallow, and easy. Relaxed.

Everything in my body had been clenched for so long, as though I was bracing for a blind-side hit that never came. But now, a few minutes after hanging up the phone—"Can you call back another time?"—I was fine. No frustration, no anxiety, no anger.

No pain.

I was sitting at the table, head in my hands, smiling. A plan was taking shape. Now I just needed to work out the details. Plan my work so I can work my plan.

I stood up, got in my truck, and took off.

It was cold but I didn't care. I had the windows rolled all the way down, blasting my music. Eminem. 50 Cent. Hard lyrics, playing loud as I circled the cloverleaf entrance ramp and got on the Turnpike northbound.

To my right, beyond the marsh grasses and the swamplands and the Hackensack River, I could see the skyline of New York. The Empire State Building, the tower under construction at One World Trade Center.

In front of me, straight as a bullet three miles up the Turnpike—I-95, a road that stretches from New England through New Jersey on its way to south Florida, same as my NFL career—I could see the stadiums. The New Meadowlands, set to open that fall, almost ready to make its debut. The wreckage of Giants Stadium, empty since the Jets beat the Bengals on a cold, windy Sunday night to clinch a playoff spot, on its way to becoming a parking lot. They broke ground for Giants Stadium in November 1972, three months after I was born. I would outlive the stadium, my home field. But not by much.

Usually, when I drove past the stadium, I would feel the anger start to rise. *How did things get to be so bad?*

But not today. On this drive, I was beaming. *Man, what a run I had.* My family got to see me play here. My friends all saw me play. I was a starting quarterback in the NFL right here. It was fantastic.

On this day, everything was good. Crazy as it sounds, knowing where I was going and what I was planning to do, I was happy. About my career, about my plan.

A few miles later, I passed the Vince Lombardi Service Area, a rest stop sharing a name with the trophy given to Super Bowl champions. Lombardi's first head coaching job was at St. Cecilia High School in Englewood, New Jersey. He's buried in Middletown.

"Winning isn't everything, it's the only thing." Lombardi was born in Brooklyn, but he sounds like a Jersey Boy to me.

Whatever it takes, right?

I was beaming now. The sun was shining, my music was blaring, and cold air was whipping in through the open windows. I wasn't wearing a jacket—what the fuck did I need a jacket for? Soon enough, I saw the first sign of my goal. It was good to have a goal again.

I was full of energy, full of adrenaline, and headed full-speed up to the George Washington Bridge.

It would all be over soon.

6

A Box of Depends and a Note

T o that point in my NFL career, I was a wild card. I was a
special teams guy with a small package of plays to run as
a quarterback. Now, I had come to a crossroads. I needed
to prove, once and for all, that I was an NFL quarterback.

Bill Parcells still thought I could play the position. Bill
Belichick wanted me out. That was no secret.

Some of the coaches would tell me, "Belichick's trying to
get you out of here, brother. He can't stand you. He doesn't
think there's a reason for you to be on this team, and he keeps
telling Parcells that."

But Parcells kept telling Belichick, "No, we're not gonna
cut him. Not yet."

That's because in camp before the 1999 season, we didn't
have a clear-cut backup quarterback to Vinny Testaverde.
The Jets traded Glenn Foley to Seattle before the draft, which
basically left them with Vinny and me.

But then they brought in Tom Tupa, who had been primarily a punter in his three seasons in New England. Tupa, though, came into the NFL as a quarterback and had been the Cardinals' starter for a couple of seasons. They also brought in Scott Zolak.

Tupa and Zolak. The two backup quarterbacks for Drew Bledsoe during my season in New England. And now Parcells was bringing them to the Jets to compete for the spot behind Vinny.

Tupa complicated things. He could be on the 45-man active game roster as a punter, which meant Parcells wouldn't have to waste a roster spot on a third-string emergency quarterback. So, if I didn't win the battle to be Vinny's backup, there might not be a roster spot for a guy who would only play special teams.

As one season preview in the *New York Post* said, "This is the most important training camp of Ray Lucas' life."

It really was. And I knew it.

So, I asked Parcells if he would let this one particular defensive assistant coach do some extra work with me. He agreed, and I wound up getting a tutorial on defensive tendencies from Eric Mangini. He was Belichick's right-hand man at the time, and you could tell how intelligent he was, how he saw the game. And after a long-ass day that started for him at 7:00 AM in the morning and went until 9:30 PM at night, he was willing to sit with me and teach me about defensive tendencies.

If I didn't make it, that was going to be my undoing. I always felt that I had the physical talent to play the position, but the mental aspect of playing quarterback at the NFL level was extremely difficult for me. When I was playing receiver, it was much easier. You can't really screw it up. Different routes had different numbers; they call the number, you run the route.

Now, I was getting playbooks every week of 150 plays, which we'd chop down to around 120. And the quarterback had to know what all 11 guys were doing on every play, as well as what the defense was doing.

So, every night, after our last position meetings, Eric would work with me one-on-one. As much as I was learning at Vinny's side, I needed more. We'd watch tape and he'd point out things I needed to start picking up on my own. "If the cornerback is standing a certain way, you know he's bailing because his hips are open. If he's lined up over here, and he opens his hips to the right and his ass is to the sideline, he's trying to force the receiver inside. He's got help inside, so it's a zone coverage."

Little things like that would be big things for me. I would go out to the practice field, step up to the line of scrimmage, and think, *Ass to the sideline. Got it.*

The film work and the scouting reports were all so sophisticated. If I wanted to know what a dude had for breakfast, Eric could have helped me figure it out. I give him a lot of credit for my career. Throwing the football becomes a whole lot easier when you know what's going on before the snap of the ball.

This was going to be my new life in the NFL. A quarterback's life.

It really didn't feel official until our first preseason game on the road. We got to our hotel, I put my key card in the door, stepped into my room, and saw just one bed.

I called the front desk immediately to complain.

"Listen. I'm in the wrong room. I don't know what's going on here, but I'm not sharing a bed with anyone."

The woman on the phone assured me that I was in the right room. And that there wouldn't be anyone else staying with me.

This couldn't be. I ran straight to Vinny's room.

"Did you know about this?"

"Of course. Quarterbacks need our space. You need time to go over the game plan in your mind."

Until then, I had always had a roommate on the road. When you're on special teams and the eighth-string wide receiver, you get a double bed next to some other guy in a double bed. He's always up when you're trying to sleep, and you're always keeping his ass up when he's trying to nap. It sucks.

But this was fantastic. No roommate. Big-ass bed to myself. Life as a quarterback. I could get used to this.

It was still, however, a backup quarterback's life. You might get your own room on one night and be on the street the next.

The day after our second preseason game, we acquired Rick Mirer from Green Bay. Zolak was gone. And it looked like the coaches felt they had found their backup.

Which made it that much more surprising when Parcells came up to me about an hour before our next preseason game and told me, "You're starting."

I couldn't figure out what he was talking about.

"Starting what?"

"What the fuck are you talking about? We're putting you behind center."

Just like that, I was starting a preseason game against the Giants.

Here's the funny part. I was still on special teams.

We kicked off to open the game, and I was out there covering the kick. We stopped them, got the ball back, and I went out there as the starting quarterback. There probably aren't too many guys in the history of the NFL who started on special teams and wound up playing quarterback in their careers. But I can't imagine *any* of them doing it in the same game.

I opened the game with our first-team offense, going against New York's first-team defense. Michael Strahan. Jesse Armstead. And we marched straight down the field on them. Thirteen plays, 77 yards. I completed all four of my passes. Curtis Martin ran one in. We were on the board.

But there was a problem. Earlier in that opening drive, Curtis fumbled the ball, and Strahan was right there, getting his hands on it. I dove right on top of him and ripped the ball away from him. No way was I going to let him come away with that loose ball. No way was I going to let that drive end with a turnover.

We kept possession. A few plays later, we scored.

My shoulder, though, didn't feel right. I dislocated it getting the ball back from Strahan.

Didn't matter. I was not taking myself out of this game. I finished the drive. Then I stayed out there for the kickoff. I even made the tackle.

When I came off the field, the first thing Parcells said to me was, "You're finished for the day."

Immediately, I got defensive.

"You can't take me out. I'm all right."

Parcells looked right at me.

"I can see your shoulder is hurt. I know it hurts. It's all right. You're done for the day. That's it."

And that was it. I spent the rest of the night on the sideline, wondering whether I'd shown him enough on that one drive against the Giants starters.

I didn't play much in the preseason finale against the Vikings, which a lot of people were predicting might be a preview of Super Bowl XXXIV. I got a couple of snaps, while Mirer played a half and pretty much locked up his spot.

The night wasn't a total loss for me. I got to meet my idol, Randall Cunningham, Minnesota's starting quarterback.

Randall was my boy. I had his poster up on my bedroom wall when I was a kid. I grew up a Cowboys fan, and I was a huge Danny White fan, but the first time I saw Randall play for the Eagles, I thought, *Ooh, where did this guy come from?* He had a cannon. I could throw the ball hard, but Randall could really bring it. And the way he played was so athletic; I still get goosebumps when I think about the time Lawrence Taylor was coming from behind to take his head off and Randall ducked and L.T. went flying past him. Randall Cunningham started the whole "running quarterback" trend—which opened the door for me. I was more like him than Dan Marino or Troy Aikman or Vinny. Plus, he was a black quarterback. I just idolized everything about him.

Both teams were coming off the field before the game, and we had just gotten into the tunnel when I felt somebody slap me on the back of the neck. A lot of fights happen in the tunnel before the game, so I whipped around and saw it was Randall. Just saying hello.

All I managed was to mumble something like, "Do you think you could give me an autograph or something?"

He smiled.

"You come see me after the game."

Sure enough, after the game, I heard someone calling, "Luke." It was Randall. He walked over to me, and on the field, right in front of everyone, he took his jersey off and handed it to me. My father was in the stands, watching this great moment happen.

Of course, I was praying Parcells didn't see this scene. I took Randall's jersey, stuffed it in my helmet, went straight into the locker room, and buried my helmet in my bag, worried that someone was going to see me with Randall Cunningham's game jersey. I took my helmet home with me to Harrison that night, with the jersey still balled up inside it. When the equipment manager called the house, wondering what I'd done with my helmet, I had to lie and tell him I'd taken it home by mistake.

It was a pretty cool experience, and a great way to kick off a season that everyone around the Jets was excited about. We knew we had a real chance to be great. We knew we had the talent. We all believed we were going to the Super Bowl.

Sometimes over the summer, quarterbacks will call the receivers together for a workout, and some don't want to come. Not this year. Everyone was all in that off-season. Starting the year as Super Bowl contenders isn't something Jets fans are used to.

I showed up for the opening game—at home against New England—and was shocked to find a T-shirt waiting for me in my locker. Before every game, there are a handful of guys whose equipment isn't laid out in their locker. They get T-shirts and hats instead. Those are the guys who are not dressing for that game.

I had a T-shirt in my locker. And I wasn't fucking sticking around. I needed to get the hell out of there.

Parcells saw me heading for the exit and asked me what I was doing.

"I'm fucking leaving. You want me to stand there on the fucking sideline with a T-shirt? I'm not doing it."

Maurice Carthon, our running backs coach, stepped between us, and he and I started chesting up. Things were getting pretty hot. Until Vinny stepped in.

"Listen, I need you," he said. "I need you to be my eyes on the sideline. I need you to see that stuff that I can't see. I need to be able to come off the field and ask you about the coverage. I need you to be my eyes."

Immediately a switch flipped inside me. It wasn't about me. It was about what my team needed me to do. My guy told me that he needed me, and that was all I needed to hear. I put on the T-shirt and the hat and went down to the field to start the season on the sideline.

Everything started out great. We scored on our first possession, a 27-yard touchdown pass from Vinny to Richie Anderson.

We were down 10–7 when we started our second possession of the second quarter on New England's 49-yard line. Vinny completed a pass to Curtis Martin for a first down. Two plays later, Curtis rushed for another first down at the Patriots' 18. We were moving the ball and about to take the lead.

Vinny handed off to Curtis, who was hit by Willie McGinest and fumbled. Vinny made a quick cut toward the loose ball and crumpled. From where I was standing, it looked like he'd been shot.

Everyone else was watching the ball, which Curtis recovered. I started pointing at Vinny, yelling, "Somebody go get him! Vinny's down!"

Vinny got up and tried to get to the sideline. Everybody knew, right away, that this was bad.

I didn't know what I should do. Leave him alone? Go talk to him? I wanted to go into the locker room with him, in case he needed anything. I just went over to him and asked a question I already knew the answer to.

"Hey, Vin, you all right?"

"No, Luke."

And he kept repeating it.

"No, Luke. No, Luke."

Tupa went into the game, and on the next play he threw a touchdown pass to Keyshawn Johnson. But I was on the sideline, in complete shock, trying to make sense of the last few minutes.

Everyone in the building was thinking the same thing: *Our season is over.* We came into that game thinking we were going to the Super Bowl. Now, a little more than one quarter into our first game, we were fucked.

We wound up losing that game 30–28. Afterward, Keyshawn was so upset he smashed the podium during his postgame press conference.

But in football, when someone goes down, there's no time to dwell on it. Everyone turns to the next man up. As hard as it is, you have to let it go and move on. It is a harsh business that way. This was my lifting partner, my lunch partner, my study partner. This was the guy who helped me prepare to become a quarterback more than anyone ever had. This was the starting quarterback on a Super Bowl–caliber team. And in Week 1, he's out for the year with a ruptured Achilles tendon.

The game goes on. And the next man up was Rick Mirer.

Things were different immediately. When Vinny was starting, we'd have our quarterback meetings with Dan Henning. Every day, we'd wrap it up with Dan asking, "Everybody good?" We'd say, "Yeah," and we'd be done and out the door.

We were finishing up the Friday meeting the first week with Rick as the starter, and Dan asked, "Everybody good?"

I said, "Yeah," and started to get up to go.

Rick was still sitting down. "Um, can I ask you something?"

He looked down at his notepad, which had two pages filled with questions about the game plan. Front and back.

Dan lost his mind. "Are you kidding me? We're supposed to be in here fine-tuning, and you still have this many questions?"

Things didn't get much better from there. We went up to Buffalo and lost 17–3. Then, we lost at home to Washington. No one was talking Super Bowl anymore. We were 0–3.

The losing was wearing on Parcells. He didn't have to say anything. You could just look at him and see something wasn't right. You knew he wasn't sleeping much. Typical Jersey boy, Parcells didn't know how to live with losing. We drive that shit around with us.

We gathered for our regular Monday meeting the day after a loss to the Jaguars dropped our record to 1–4. All the quarterbacks sat up front, as usual. Vinny was there, too; he was still hanging around the complex, getting treatment.

Parcells walked into the room and everyone got quiet. He pointed at the front row.

"This fucking kid is starting. I don't care if we lose every game. Either you get behind him or you don't."

I turned around to see who he was pointing at. I spotted Vinny, looking at me, laughing.

"He's talking about you."

I still wasn't processing what just happened.

"Luke, you're the starter."

Of course, the first thing I had to do was call my wife. I ran straight downstairs, passed by my locker, and noticed someone had left something for me: a box of Depends with a note that read, "Try not to shit your pants. —Coach."

It was just what I needed to put my mind at ease. All the chaos in my head after hearing the news was gone.

A little while later, I had a meeting with Parcells. He was trying to make sure I would approach my new role the right way.

"Don't worry. I am going to put you in the best position for you to be successful. Don't feel like you have to do too much right away."

Which was nice to hear, since until then I only had to worry about my three plays. Now, we were talking about the whole enchilada.

"Don't be shy about throwing the football away. If you don't like what you're seeing, throw it away. Now, you're going to have to be a leader."

It sounded like he was finished, so I said, "Got it," and got up to leave.

"Whoa, whoa. Where are you going?"

I sat back down, and wound up hearing one of the key lessons I still needed to learn.

"It doesn't matter if I say you're the leader. You're not a leader until you earn it from those 10 guys in the huddle with you."

That gave me pause. How does a special teams guy walk into a huddle and command respect? How am I going to earn it?

During that first week of practice, we were working on red zone situations. I was in the huddle, trying to call a play. Parcells was a few yards behind me, talking to one of the other coaches. My guys couldn't hear me.

I don't know what possessed me to say this, or how I let the words out of my mouth, but I whipped around and snapped at Parcells: "Would you please shut the fuck up?"

You know how you sometimes see words floating out of your mouth like a comic strip balloon? And you try to reel them back in but you can't? That was one of those moments.

"What did you just say to me?"

I started fast-talking. "I'm trying to call the plays over here, and you're talking over there, and everybody's saying 'What? What?' because they can't hear me because you're talking too loud. And if we screw up, you're going to yell at me, and it's all because they can't hear me."

He looked me straight in the eye and said, "If you ever talk to me like that again, there won't be a fucking piece of lint left in your locker."

I spun around, lowered my head, went right back to the huddle, and started calling the next play.

Then I heard him say to the rest of the team, "If I had 10 more guys like this kid, we wouldn't lose one fucking game."

After practice, Curtis Martin pulled me aside and told me, "That was the moment."

That was the moment when my teammates bought in. That's the moment they thought, *We can get behind this kid.*

My first NFL start was against Indianapolis. And Peyton Manning.

I stood there on the sideline, listening to him call a play, and I could not understand what the fuck he was doing. I was getting a headache trying to sort through all the verbiage I heard him yelling.

I didn't find out until much later that 70 percent of everything Peyton does in pre-snap is bullshit. He was like a magician, waving his hands around, trying to get the defense to watch something that wasn't important. "Watch my hands. Listen to what I'm saying. Pay no attention to that receiver over there, where I'm really going with the ball." And all the time he was processing information on how to beat you.

Everything started off great. We marched downfield on our first series; John Hall missed a field goal. The Colts went three and out, we got the ball back, marched right down again, Hall kicked a field goal, we're up 3–0. Victor Green picked off Peyton; four plays later, another field goal. We're up 6–0.

On our next possession, we scored a touchdown—a short pass to Richie Anderson, who was probably the most gifted pass catcher of any running back in the league at the time. He took it 18 yards for my first touchdown pass in the NFL.

Twenty-six minutes into my first NFL start, it's Jets 13, Colts 0. Peyton Manning: 1-for-5 for five yards and an interception. Ray Lucas: 12-for-16, 112 yards, one touchdown, plus another nine yards rushing.

Unfortunately, we didn't score again.

We did have a shot, though. We got the ball at midfield with under eight minutes left in the game and the score tied

13–13. I'd thrown three straight incompletions on our last possession, so we rode Curtis Martin on this series. Five straight runs by Curtis and we had 1st-and-goal from the Colts' 3.

My pass was intended for Keyshawn Johnson, but it was late. Jeff Burris intercepted it at the goal line and returned it 55 yards. Four and a half minutes later, Mike Vanderjagt kicked a 27-yard game-winner.

But the game wasn't over.

We had the ball on our 20 with nine seconds left. There was enough time for us to run a couple of desperation plays. First, I threw an incompletion, a pass intended for Keyshawn. Then the game ended on a sack. I was scrambling around, trying to make something happen, and Ellis Johnson got me. My foot got stuck in the ground, my leg went one way, and Johnson wound up on my leg. I heard something snap.

On the last play of my first NFL start, I fractured the skinny bone in my ankle.

They called it a high ankle sprain. I tried to go that next week in Oakland, even though I hadn't taken a rep in practice during the week. They were giving me treatment on the flight, and I took a couple of Vicodin before we went out on the field for warmups. I was throwing the ball pretty well and I wasn't limping—at least not to the point where anybody would notice. Every once in a while, I got a flash of hot pain that would shoot all the way up my leg. But I told Parcells, "I can go. If you need me, I'm here."

I dressed, but I didn't play against the Raiders (a 24–23 loss), even though I know Maurice Carthon was on the sideline telling Parcells to put me in. After the bye week, I also missed the Arizona game (a 12–7 win).

But I was ready to go in Week 10, and I got the start. At New England. Against Pete Carroll. On *Monday Night Football.*

But first I needed to convince Parcells to do something he never did.

Parcells never took injured players on the road. He felt there was no reason for them to be there, that there was nothing they could do on the sideline but be a distraction. Belichick has that policy to this day: if you're injured, you don't travel.

But I needed Vinny there. I needed him to be my eyes on the sideline. I needed to be able to come over after a series and talk to him about coverages.

That Vinny wanted to come, and even lobbied Parcells himself, meant a lot to me. He knew I was an emotional guy, and he wanted to be there to help me keep everything in check, to reel me back in if necessary.

A quarterback needs to have amnesia; he can't let one bad play become two. Let's say he almost throws an interception on one play, and he starts thinking about it: *Did I throw it too early? Did the cornerback do something I never saw him do on film?* If he starts doing that, he's screwed.

The first time he gets hit in the face, if he thinks about it too long, he'll stop looking downfield and start peeking in at the line of scrimmage, just to make sure there's nobody sneaking through. Now, his next pass is late, too. Another negative play. One becomes two. We become our own worst enemy.

Nobody sees that battle going on inside a quarterback's head. We have to think about so many things on every play, if a negative thought starts creeping in, we have to send that bitch right back out. Otherwise, things are going to go sideways. Especially for a young, emotional quarterback like me.

Vinny knew he could help me stay under control.

I begged Parcells, and he agreed. Vinny, walking boot and all, would get to travel with us to New England.

That Monday night, I could do no wrong out there against the Patriots. They couldn't touch me.

We scored three times in the second quarter—I threw one touchdown pass to Keyshawn, one to Fred Baxter, and Curtis scored one in between. The whole time, I kept trying to get to the Patriots sideline, just so I could yell at Pete Carroll.

I got close enough once, and couldn't resist asking him a question:

"How about now? Am I good enough to play in this league now, motherfucker?"

We wound up winning 24–17 in the most gratifying game of my entire career. Of my entire life. In any sport. That was the pinnacle, to be able to go back and stick it up the ass of the guy who cut me.

Cecy was back home in Jersey, watching that game with her doctor from a hospital bed. She was pregnant with our second daughter, Madison, and had been put on bed rest. The doc worked to keep her calm throughout the game, but she was probably even more nervous when she saw me getting interviewed after the game. Cecy knew that there was a good chance some vengeful shit would come out of my mouth that probably shouldn't be said on TV.

That was another lesson Vinny taught me: "Never go straight into the room."

He knew how emotional I could be. And he reminded me that I needed to get it together and keep it together before I met the media. That's part of the job of a starting quarterback.

"No matter how good you play, no matter how bad you play. Sit down, calm down, and collect your thoughts before you talk to them."

That might not sound like a big deal, but it was crucial to me. On top of everything I learned from Vinny about playing the position, he taught me how to be a professional.

I managed to keep myself in check during that interview on the field at the old Foxboro Stadium. The reporter asked me about Pete Carroll, and I didn't give her anything more than, "I guess he's gonna have to sleep on that tonight."

When the interview wrapped and the crew moved on, I started jogging toward the visitor's locker room on the left side of the end zone. At the top of the ramp leading down to the locker room, I saw one person standing alone waiting for me. In a boot.

Vinny.

I ran straight over to him and hugged him, and I lost it. He told me he was proud of me, that he was just as excited as I was.

Most people don't ever get to experience a moment like that. He was my mentor, my friend. He taught me everything. He knew how long I had waited and how hard I had worked for the chance to have a night like this. We got there together.

To have had the chance to share that moment with Vinny is something I will never forget.

7

Fantasyland

For eight games—half a football season—I was a starting quarterback in the NFL.

It was awesome. People were wearing Ray Lucas jerseys to the games. The first time I went into Modell's and saw they were selling No. 6 Jets jerseys, I started crying my eyes out. It was insane.

People would drop by the house to wish me luck or get an autograph. Everybody in town was along for the ride.

Game day was huge. Every week, we'd scramble to find tickets for everybody who wanted to come to the game. Giants Stadium is about nine miles from Harrison, and we'd have to beg all the guys from out of town for tickets they weren't going to use, just so we could take care of everyone. I didn't know who was coming each week; I just knew that they were going to be my people, and a lot of them.

Cecy would oversee the whole game day routine. "How many do we have today? Twenty-six? Got it." She loved coming to the game. Whenever I would do something exciting, she would throw her shoulders back, all nice and proud, and say, "Yeah, that's my guy."

I think she probably enjoyed the game more when I wasn't out on the field. When I was in the game, she was on edge. She'd be sitting in the family section—under the overhang, so she'd be covered in the snow or rain—focusing just on me. She wanted to see for herself that I would get up at the end of every play. It couldn't have been easy to watch her husband get rocked, then search for a sign that I was okay once I got to the sideline. Then, when I'd go in for the next series, she'd be pissed off at me: "Didn't we just have this talk last week? Can't you sit out just a little longer?"

She knew the answer. I was not sitting down. Not now. Not while that job was mine.

For those two months, I wasn't worrying about getting cut, about whether I was going to dress. About playing special teams. All I had to do was focus on the challenge of playing and developing as a quarterback. Finally, after all these years, I was getting a chance to work my craft. I was behind the center, with the first team, getting the physical reps to go with the mental reps.

And I had so much help.

I had Charlie Weis as my offensive coordinator, and he was great. The whole nature of our play-calling had to change once I became the starter. Vinny Testaverde was a true pocket quarterback. If the plan had been for me to drop back 30 times, we weren't going to win that game. I had to get out on the corner, so Charlie brought in a lot of sprint passes. More quarterback draws were installed into our game plan. The option came in. Can you imagine, a Parcells team running the option? We added rollouts, moving the pocket all the time. I was doing things pretty much no one else was doing at that time. As Parcells had promised, Charlie put me in the best possible situations to succeed.

And I had Dan Henning as my quarterbacks coach. Dan was laid-back but he'd get on your ass if he had to. More than anything else, Dan was a technician, and I learned so much about the technique required to play quarterback from Dan. He taught me about throwing the deep ball properly, that it should be thrown on a high arc and then drop out of the sky like a raindrop into the receiver's hands.

Dan had a metal frame constructed, with poles sticking up from it in all directions to simulate a wall of defensive linemens' hands going up to knock down your pass. In the off-season, he would have us drop back and throw against this contraption. He'd put buckets down on the field 40 yards away, and we'd have to drop back, keep our eyes downfield, find the passing lane, and put the ball in the bucket.

It certainly helped my development that in practice I got to go against our defense, which was always so prepared because of Bill Belichick. We had Mo Lewis, Aaron Glenn, Jason Ferguson. Marvin Jones was a monster. Victor Green would come turn your facemask sideways on you. Just a nasty defense to go against. I loved it. It made me better.

People always say that Belichick's a genius, and they're right. Going up against him every day and watching him work up close was amazing. He just knows everything. During my first couple of seasons with him, when I was just playing special teams, the defense would come over to the sideline and gather around Belichick. I was like a little kid, running over to listen in, to hear what he talked to them about. I saw him throw out an entire defensive game plan one series into the game and draw up a new one right there on the sideline.

I always wanted Belichick's respect, and, like with Parcells, that doesn't come easy. Guys like that don't give it out freely; you have to earn it.

Three weeks after the Monday night game in New England, we played the Giants. We lost 41–28, but I had a big game: 31-for-48, 284 yards, four touchdowns, no interceptions. I was sitting at my locker after that game, and Belichick came by and said, "Good game, Ray."

I was floored. He had never said anything like that to me before. It took four years to hear him say that. When you're a Parcells Guy, it's like you're a made guy in the Mafia. Still, to hear the Captain, the Capo, come over and tell you straight up, "Good game"? You hear that and everything you're doing—the lifting, the studying, the coming in at 7:00 AM and going home at 9:00 PM, the ice treatments—it's all worth it.

And, of course, I had Parcells, who believed in me. Who made me believe in me. Parcells was a master of the Xs and Os, but more than that, he was a master manipulator of the mind. He got you to buy into yourself, into what he believed you were capable of doing. Every time I was under center, I had all the confidence in the world in my ability. In reality, more than I probably should have. But I believed because of Parcells. More than anyone other than my father, there was no man more important in my life than Bill Parcells.

You either loved playing for him or you hated it; there was no middle ground. If you hated it, you still probably played your ass off for him just to make sure he didn't rip you to shreds. At the same time, if you played well and he didn't talk to you, you were still shitting your pants, wondering why he wasn't talking to you at all.

Parcells is the kind of guy who would take you to a cliff and tell you to hang off of it. Then he'd step on one of your hands, to see if you could hold on. If you could, he would pick you up and put you behind him, with the other guys who hung on. That's the kind of thing it took to be a Parcells Guy. There was that never-ending test of your mental toughness, your physical toughness. He had to know: "Can I count on you when the situation is dire? Can I trust you to step up and answer the call?"

That's how a special teams guy wound up as a starting quarterback. That just doesn't happen. And I knew it had everything to do with those coaches and with the guys I had standing in front of me, behind me, to the left and the right of me. I had it all.

My offensive linemen were killers. Kevin Mawae was the center. He was a Christian, with a cross taped to the front of his facemask, but he was a different boy when you crossed over that line. He must have gone to confession every Sunday night after talking as much shit as he did on the field. Then there was Jumbo Elliott. He'd put his helmet on and immediately want to kill whoever was lined up in front of him. Even in practice. Didn't matter. He was 325 pounds and had 12-pack abs; Jumbo was an absolute monster.

I loved having all my big fatties over to the house every Thursday for dinner. I knew I couldn't do for them what other quarterbacks could do for their linemen—buy them Rolexes or some fancy gifts. I couldn't even afford to take them out to dinner every week; they would've broke me. So, Cecy made a shitload of chicken parmigiana and pasta or my mom would make lasagna, and we'd have my guys over to eat at our place. Cecy always worried that she was making too much food; it never turned out to be enough. Not with those guys. Not with Randy Thomas around. He was a rookie that year; my god, could he eat.

I had Freddie Baxter, my tight end. I had Dedric Ward, one of my best friends, who was so fast, totally unafraid to go over the middle. I had Curtis Martin, Hall of Famer. I had Richie Anderson, probably the best fullback in the game at the time. Tough, versatile.

I had Wayne Chrebet. Garfield High School. Jersey boy. I was like Linus with his security blanket when Chrebet was out there. I knew I could count on him to be open anywhere.

I had Keyshawn Johnson. He would come into the huddle and tell me, "Luke, I'm open."

I'd say, "Key, I didn't even call the play yet."

"I don't care what play it is. I'm open."

What more could you ask for than a guy like that, who wants the ball on every play, who believes he's going to win his battle and get open? Keyshawn was tough and was never afraid to throw a block downfield. He ran great routes, had great body control in the air, great hands. He was the best.

And, of course, I still had Vinny. No one was more important for my success and my sanity. He was always the buffer between me and Parcells. I would come to the sideline and Parcells would rip my ass apart. Then I'd go sit down with Vinny, look at the pictures, and say, "Tell me what I did wrong."

For those precious weeks, life was everything I dreamed it could be. I was living in Fantasyland.

The Sunday before Christmas, we went to Dallas. I was a huge Cowboys fan as a kid. My parents have a picture of me walking around in some tighty-whiteys and a 10-gallon hat and cowboy boots. Black cowboy boots. Great look for the only black kid in town.

My father was a die-hard Giants fan. So were all his friends. They all had season tickets to the Giants games, and they'd take me whenever Dallas was in town.

I was a cocky little kid, running around, teasing everyone because the Cowboys never lost in those days. One time, they chased me and they caught me. They made me take off my Cowboys shirt, and they started the grill with it. I was standing outside in December, no shirt, freezing my ass off, and my dad said, "If you're gonna run your mouth, that's what's gonna happen."

I loved Tony Dorsett and Danny White and Randy White. Too Tall Jones and Everson Walls. I was a crazy Cowboys fan.

And there I was in Dallas in 1999—as a starting quarterback.

Troy Aikman was there. Emmitt Smith was there. Deion Sanders was there.

I went over to Texas Stadium and into the locker room for my pregame ritual, which included laying out my jersey and pants on the floor, with the pads in them. I had a huge dip in, and I was going over my plan for the day. I plan my work, then I work my plan.

I got dressed and went out on the field alone. I walked straight to midfield and laid down right in the middle of the star. I closed my eyes and took it all in, the only time in my career I'd ever done anything like that. I never appreciated the game while I was playing it; that's the one thing I regret to this day. But that morning in Dallas, I was so lost in my own world, I hadn't heard people coming out around me. Not until someone standing above me said, "Excuse me."

I opened my eyes. It was one of the Dallas Cowboys cheerleaders. I just smiled and said, "God, you can take me right now if you want."

During the game, I kept throwing at Deion's side of the field. Parcells called me over to the sideline and asked, "What the fuck are you doing?"

"I don't care who they have over there. I'm going by what my reads tell me, just like we worked on."

"Well, you throw a pick to that guy and you'll be watching the rest of the game from over here."

In the third quarter, I did throw a pick—but the pass was intercepted by Randall Godfrey, not Deion. I did lead an 11-play drive late in the fourth quarter that ended with John Hall's game-winning field goal.

I had come to Dallas and won as a starting quarterback. We went home with our second straight win.

Things were starting to slow down for me. I was finding my comfort zone. I would walk through the tunnel and onto the field, and I felt like there was nothing the defense could do that I wasn't ready for. I almost wanted to laugh when things played out as we had prepared. I would drop back, see the safety move, and think, *I knew he was going to do that.* I'd notice the linebacker had his right foot forward instead of his left, and I knew that meant he was going to blitz. So, I'd go out and dog it a bit, let him think that I hadn't picked up on anything. Then, just as he was about to blitz, I'd throw it hot—right where they didn't want me to. They thought they had me but I had them all along.

I was getting practice reps with my receivers, developing the kind of chemistry you need to succeed. I could throw the ball before my guy would break out of his cut; I knew exactly where he was going to be. That's comfort. That's trust. And it starts to become second nature.

It's like having the answers to the test. "There is nothing you can do to keep me from kicking your ass." I felt bulletproof.

Which, of course, I wasn't.

• • •

The one thing you could never prepare for was the blind-side shot. The shots you don't see coming. Those are the ones that can end you.

I was never afraid of getting hit. I loved to run the ball in short-yardage situations, even though I knew I was going to get hit. I'd get the first down and start jumping around and going crazy, like I'd just run for 50 yards. Or I'd be on the bottom of the pile, talking shit to the defense: "Is that really the best you can do? If that's all you got, next time, I won't even bother to move out of the way. I'll just let you hit me."

Not everyone was like that. Curtis Martin would be on the bottom of the pile, and the defense would be talking shit to him. Curt would just say, "God bless you." What could they say to that?

I would talk even when they did get me good. That was my defense mechanism. Sometimes, you would take a shot you never saw coming, you'd see stars in front of your eyes, and think, for one second, *Is this worth it?* But I wasn't going to let anybody know they beat me. Maybe it was the Jersey in me. I would rather people think I was crazy than know that in reality I couldn't feel my shoulder.

Vinny would always encourage me to slide, rather than initiate contact. But I just wasn't a slider. Eventually it started to dawn on me that if I wanted to stay in this game, unnecessary hits are best to be avoided.

Because people are trying to kill the quarterback. No joke.

Rules about hitting the quarterback were different when I played than they are today. When I played, a guy could put his helmet right in the middle of a quarterback's back. A good blind-side shot was a chance to put me on the sideline. It was a part of the game, and it was accepted by everyone. Even quarterbacks.

Probably the worst blind-side shot I ever took was against Miami, the week before we went to Dallas. Daryl Gardener played nose tackle for the Dolphins. Apart from Jumbo, he was one of the biggest human beings I'd ever seen. I remembered first seeing him at the combine when we were both coming out of college; he was so big, he had to sit across two chairs.

Parcells always wanted his quarterbacks to be like the mailman—rain, sleet, snow, whatever, you have to deliver the mail. We had to be prepared to stand in there and take a hit if need be to deliver the ball.

I was in the pocket, getting ready to throw a quick out to Wayne Chrebet in the slot. I got the ball out, and at the last second, I turned my head. Unfortunately it wasn't soon enough to see Gardner coming from my back side. Then the lights went out.

My linemen were gathered around, trying to get me up off the turf, but I told them I needed a minute. At least, that's what I tried to tell them. I found out later that I was trying to speak but I was slurring my words. I didn't understand at the time why my teammates were laughing at me; apparently, I was trying to talk but it was coming out gibberish.

Elliot Pellman, the team doctor, told me to get up, that I was embarrassing him. So, I popped up and went over to the sideline. Even though I had no idea where I was.

They didn't ask me too many questions on the sideline. There was no "*Cat. Dog. Horse.* Now, repeat to me the three words I just told you." There was no, "List the months of the year." Parcells asked me, "What's Play 4?" I told him, and they sent me back into the game.

I missed one snap.

And on my first snap back in the game, I threw a 24-yard touchdown to Keyshawn. It broke a 13–13 tie and gave us the lead for good in a game we won 28–20.

Ironically, the play I was hurt on never officially happened. I completed the pass to Chrebet, but there were off-setting penalties on the play. Gardener got flagged for roughing the passer. Richie Anderson got a penalty for an illegal block above the waist.

Daryl Gardener nearly retired me on a play that turned out to be a do-over.

Two weeks later, we saw Gardener and the Dolphins again. Another *Monday Night Football* game, this time in Miami. Against Dan Marino.

Early in the game, I would be at the line, making adjustments, and Dolphins linebacker Zach Thomas would be calling our plays out: "They're coming this way. They're running in this hole."

I went to Parcells, who called our plays, and told him, "Coach, this guy knows everything we're doing. He's calling our plays."

"Oh yeah?" Parcells said. "Next time we get the ball, I want you to go out there and tell him *exactly* what we're running. If we can execute it, he can't stop it."

So, the next time out, I did just what Parcells told me.

"Hey, Zach. We're going right here. Can you stop it?"

We ran the ball where I told him we would. Four-yard gain.

"Zach, we're going this way this time. You might want to move over."

Five-yard gain.

"Shut the fuck up."

It was a close game throughout, and we took the lead in the third quarter on a 50-yard touchdown pass to Chrebet. I saw that Miami was in man coverage, that there would be no safety help. So, I watched the cornerback to see if he was going to sit on Chrebet's first move. As soon as he sat, I knew it was over. I got rid of the ball before he made his second move.

I was executing the way a quarterback is supposed to. I learned from Dan Henning to backpedal every time I was going to throw to my left; dropping back sideways means you have to get your hips out of the way. It complicates the throw. I was learning.

The Dolphins were still in the hunt for a playoff berth, and they needed this win. With about nine minutes left, Olindo Mare missed a 54-yard field goal that would've tied the game. We took over at our own 44-yard line.

They always pumped music into Pro Player Stadium during TV timeouts, and everyone in the crowd was dancing. I was furious.

In the huddle, I yelled at my guys.

"Everybody turn around right now. Take a look at these fucking people."

They all turned around. They were listening to me. One Chief, 10 Indians.

"They all think they're gonna come back on us. They think they've got us. It's time to put the last nail in the coffin."

The play came in from the sideline; we were going to take our shot. Parcells was the kind of coach who loved to go for broke after a change of possession like that. Loss of downs. Turnover. A missed field goal. When our opponents gave him a chance, he wanted to break their spirit right away.

We ran a play-action fake to Curtis. Down the right sideline, Dedric Ward ran right past Terrell Buckley, who thought he had safety help over the top. You can see it in the replays; he threw up his hands when he turned and saw Shawn Wooden wasn't where he was supposed to be. That's because I had looked Wooden off to my left.

It turned into a 56-yard touchdown pass, my third of the night. We beat the Dolphins and moved to one game under .500.

In seven weeks, I had wins against Dan Marino and Drew Bledsoe on *Monday Night Football*. Plus a road win against Troy Aikman. Two quarterbacks taken No. 1 in the draft. Two Hall of Famers. And if I hadn't thrown that pick against Indianapolis, I'd have had a win against Peyton Manning, too.

Me. The kid from special teams.

By the time we beat Seattle in Week 17, we were probably one of the hottest teams in football. We'd won four in a row and seven of nine—six of the eight straight games I started at quarterback. The team that started 1–6 and lost its starting quarterback in the first half of the first game was 8–8 and on a roll.

Nobody would've wanted to play us in the playoffs—if we'd made it. We didn't. One break here or there (that fucking pick in Indianapolis), we would've gone to the playoffs, and everything might have been different. Years later, Parcells would say it was the best coaching job of his career.

I didn't want the season to end. I had proven I could play and win in the NFL.

Everyone expected Vinny would be back next year. I'd be back to holding a clipboard.

At least I could count on what Parcells had told me. "If you play well," he'd said after he'd given me the starting job, "you won't have anything to worry about."

8

Shot

The bad news announced itself on my caller ID.

NEW YORK JETS.

I knew that couldn't be good.

I was home with Rayven, watching the NFL Draft, while Cecy was in the hospital, losing weight and still on bed rest, waiting to deliver our second baby.

The Jets had four picks in the first round that year, and we'd already used two: Shaun Ellis and John Abraham, picks No. 12 and 13. We were coming up again at No. 18.

I didn't answer the call from the Jets office. Instead, I called my agent and told him something was up.

"I need you to find out what the fuck is going on."

I had my answer before he called me back. I got it from ESPN.

"With the 18th pick of the 2000 NFL Draft, the New York Jets select Chad Pennington, quarterback, Marshall."

All the air immediately went out of my body. My agent and I were in contract negotiations with the Jets at the time, and suddenly everything changed.

Actually, everything had already changed.

The day after our season-ending win over Seattle, Parcells resigned. As soon as I heard the news, I went to his office and begged him to stay for one more year. We were so close. We were half a game from the Super Bowl two seasons earlier. We lost Vinny in our first game in 1999 and still rallied and almost made the playoffs. But he'd had it, for a lot of reasons, and was going up to the front office.

Bill Belichick quickly was named our new head coach.

At the introductory press conference, Belichick, too, resigned. After one day. He'd handwritten his letter of resignation on a piece of scrap paper: "I resign as HC of the NYJ."

Two weeks later, Woody Johnson bought the Jets.

We were all in the building one day the following week, still wondering who our head coach was going to be. Everyone expected Maurice Carthon to get the job. We left the building before any announcement had been made, and found out later that day that the new head coach was going to be Al Groh. Parcells was going to stick around in the front office, but no one at the time knew what his role would be or how long he'd be in it.

A few days later, Belichick was hired by the Patriots.

It had already been an absolutely insane off-season. And now the Jets had drafted a quarterback in the first round. It turned out I wasn't going to be taken care of the way I'd been promised.

Everything was different, except for one thing—I went into training camp having to fight for my job.

In purely business terms, the NFL stands for Not For Long. There is always somebody younger, stronger, faster, or cheaper coming along to replace you. Pennington wasn't stronger or faster than I was, and he certainly wasn't cheaper. I was making nothing compared to what he'd get as a first-round pick. For a long time, I'd jokingly ask him, "When are you gonna give me my money? You owe me $3 million."

But Chad Pennington was different than those other guys who had been brought in to challenge me for a lot of reasons. First, he was brilliant. He was probably the best quarterback I've ever been around in terms of film work. Our full playbook was five inches thick. It took me a couple of years before I was completely comfortable with everything in it. Chad was ready in about two weeks. I never saw him bring the playbook to work; he had everything in his head. He'd ask Dan Henning questions even Dan couldn't answer. Chad was incredibly smart, which was the biggest reason he was so successful.

That just meant I had to work even harder to earn my spot.

That off-season, I was more dedicated than ever about getting my mind and body ready for training camp. One day, Vinny and I were working out, doing hang cleans with about 400 pounds. The first lift went up easy; it felt like I was doing 135 pounds. Everybody in the room was cheering me on, pushing me to do one more. I went for a second lift, and as soon as I jerked the bar up, the leather strap wrapped around my right wrist and the bar snapped. My hand slipped along the bar, and everything toppled.

Pop! Pop!

I heard a sickening sound in my lower back, and I couldn't breathe. It was probably just a few seconds, but it felt like I couldn't take a breath for three minutes.

I panicked. Our strength coach Johnny Lott—the best strength coach I ever had and one of the guys who used to come to those Thursday dinners at my house in Harrison—was panicking. Strength coaches lose their jobs over things like this. Everybody in the room was panicking.

Johnny told me to lie down, but I couldn't.

"I gotta go to the training room," I told him, weakly.

No one ever asks to go to the training room unless they have to. When you were in the training room, your teammates treated you like a leper. They looked at you like you were contagious, like you had some kind of communicable disease. Some guys wouldn't even walk near you; they were afraid your shit would rub off on them.

That's because professional athletes—not just football players—are superstitious idiots. Not everyone. But anyone who is superstitious is 100 percent superstitious.

I was superstitious about my pregame ritual. I had been doing the exact same thing since high school, and I knew that if I did something the wrong way, I'd be fucked that day. If I realized that I'd forgotten to put on my right shoe first, forget it. It was over.

Superstitions are rampant in the NFL, especially when it comes to injuries. And if you were one of those guys in the ice tub all the time, no one would come near you.

But this was different. I needed to get to the training room. At first, I wasn't going to tell anybody else what happened. I wasn't going to get anybody in trouble.

Eventually, the pain became so overwhelming that I had to get an MRI. The results were not good: two herniated discs in my lower back. They had inverted, which meant they were pushing in instead of out, and they were pressing on my sciatic nerve.

The doctors gave me a choice: I could have surgery to fix it and never play football again, or I could choose to play with it and work on making everything around the discs stronger. They warned me that if I chose to play and got hit hard enough or in the wrong spot, I could be paralyzed.

In my mind, there was no decision to make.

"I don't give a shit. I'm playing. Let's go."

We had turmoil on the sideline. I was going to have to earn my spot against a guy the team had just used a first-round pick on. I was recovering from my back injury.

And things didn't get a whole lot better once training camp started.

• • •

When guys got to camp, one of the conditioning drills was a series of timed 300-yard runs. We would come in a day early, when coaches weren't allowed to be with us at practice. Usually, teams leave it up to the captains to make sure we got it done on our own.

When we arrived in 2000, Al Groh was down in the practice bubble with us, waiting for us to run. The captains told him he couldn't be there.

"I'm the head coach."

Didn't matter. The captains told him that as long as he was there, we weren't running.

It wasn't even our first official day of practice, and already we had problems. Everyone knew right away it wasn't going to be the same without Parcells in charge. But this all felt wrong.

Parcells was still in the building, serving as the team's general manager. And we had a lot of the same coaches and staff members from the year before. But things were different. One hundred percent different.

Later during training camp, a reporter asked me how I felt about my contract negotiations, my role, the transition, Pennington, everything. I told him how upset I was, how Parcells had promised to take care of me, and how things didn't happen the way I'd been told they would.

Al called me into his office after he heard about my comments, and he lectured me.

"You can't talk to the paper about things like that."

I lost it on Al, and I bounced.

I don't know how Vinny found out about it so fast, but I was barely back in my room before he was banging on my door. I could tell he was pissed.

"What did you say to him?" he demanded.

"I don't know, Vin."

I had erupted, didn't even think about what I was saying, and left. I told him as best as I could remember, and he stormed off to see Al. I don't know what Vinny said to him, but I was never told by Al Groh that I couldn't do something ever again.

I appreciated that Vinny had stood up for me, especially because I was growing short on allies. For the longest time, I wouldn't speak to Parcells. I couldn't forgive him for not taking care of me the way he told me he would.

When we broke camp, Vinny was the starter, I was No. 2, and Chad was No. 3. But the writing was on the wall. My days with the Jets were numbered.

I took snaps at quarterback in only five games during the 2000 season, and saw extended action only against Pittsburgh and Oakland, filling in when Vinny got hurt in each game. I never found a rhythm and wound up throwing a couple of interceptions against both the Steelers and the Raiders.

Eric Allen picked off the last pass I threw as a Jets quarterback. He intercepted it, I made the tackle, and then I walked off the field. On our next possession, Chad took his first snaps in the NFL. He was sacked on his first play; five plays later, he threw a touchdown pass to Wayne Chrebet.

I never saw the field again in a Jets uniform.

The following March, I signed with the Miami Dolphins as a restricted free agent for the best money I'd ever made: a three-year deal potentially worth up to $2.75 million, including an $800,000 signing bonus. Finally, I was getting paid like a quarterback—like a backup quarterback, maybe, but it was a lot better than a back-of-the-roster special teams guy. The Jets had a chance to match Miami's offer. Parcells had left after one season as general manager. Groh was gone, off to be the head coach at Virginia. The new regime, including head coach Herm Edwards, didn't match it, as I knew they wouldn't.

The only other team that expressed interest in me when I hit the market? The Patriots. Led by none other than Bill Belichick.

• • •

A few months before signing with Miami, we had moved from Harrison into a house we had built in Howell. It took a year until it was ready for the four of us—me, Cecy, Rayven, and our newest joy, Madison. We were there for a couple of months at the most, and then we had to move to Florida.

Cecy wanted to keep the house and rent a small place in Miami; that way, we'd always be able to come home in the off-season, she said. Then someone pointed out that meant we'd be coming back to Jersey for the winter. That was the end of that discussion.

I'd been promising her, "Someday, baby," for a long time. And now, with that signing bonus, I was finally making enough money that Cecy didn't need to work.

I found us a home in a gated community, with two dolphins painted on the bottom of the pool in the complex. I figured it had to be a sign. I was meant to be in Miami, right?

Of course, I had to have the car to go with it. I went out and bought my Mercedes S500.

We made all the mistakes that people with newfound wealth could have made. But, hell, this was what we had been waiting for. I'd been watching Vinny get a check for $180,000 every two weeks. You hang around guys getting paid all that money and you covet what they have. The big house. The nice car. The dolphins painted in the pool.

Our new house was always clean. My girls had whatever they wanted. Cecy and I came from nothing, and now we were going to live the good life for as long as we could. It was bliss.

Besides, I was going to play forever.

At the very least, I figured I had another eight to 10 years of holding a clipboard ahead of me, making decent money doing it. If my back would let me.

It has always amazed me that I was able to pass the physical in Miami with two herniated discs in my back. I was nervous going into that exam, knowing it could be the one thing that might blow up the deal. When I walked in, they told me to touch my toes. I held my breath, smashed my toes real good, and they signed me.

Right away, I went to work, doing the same things I'd been doing with Vinny. I was pushing 110-pound dumbbells on the flat bench when my new strength coach came over.

"What are you doing?"

"What do you mean? Am I doing something wrong?"

"No. I mean, why are you doing this? You're a quarterback, not a middle linebacker."

"Well, this is what I've always done."

"Listen, I heard about your back. It happened because you're lifting weight you shouldn't. You're a quarterback. There's no reason for you to be pressing that much weight."

So, we struck a compromise. I would lighten up on the loads I was lifting—but I wasn't going all the way down to the 35-pound dumbbells like he wanted. Hell, no.

Still, what he said made complete sense at the time. Maybe I didn't need to be a professional bodybuilder at the quarterback position.

Then my trainer asked if I'd ever done yoga. I laughed at him.

"What about Pilates?"

"Dude, I don't even know what that is."

He suggested I try it, that it would help with my back. I knew I was one good shot away from the end of my career—or worse—so I figured I'd give it a go.

I went to a studio that was set up in a rehab facility, and the only other people in the class were a bunch of old ladies. The instructor, a tiny little girl, introduced herself and told me we were going to start with Pilates, then move on to some yoga stretching.

"Whatever you say. I'm ready."

I was not ready.

She got on a Pilates machine, which is like a bench with a bunch of bands and cables attached, and started showing me all the exercises. And she talked the entire time.

"You want to keep your back straight when you do these. Make sure to breathe in through your nose and out through your mouth."

She just talked and repped them out, like it was nothing. Then it was my turn.

Oh my god.

It was fucking impossible. I had to hold my breath to do anything. She did eight reps and never stopped talking. I did three and thought I was going to pass out.

I came to take Pilates very seriously, as seriously as I took lifting with Vinny. I learned that the core is the most important part of your body. It's the center of the universe for any human being, and Pilates and yoga concentrate on developing your core muscles. And those muscles support your back, which I didn't know before I started doing Pilates. I went four times a week for four or five months, and I was back in top physical condition. Even my back felt like it was getting better.

It certainly wasn't getting overused during the 2001 season. I spent most of the year carrying the clipboard, backing up Jay Fiedler. I got into a handful of games, the first coming in Week 5 in our first game against the Jets. On our first possession, I came in on 3rd-and-1 and ran a quarterback draw for two yards. I got up jumping around, just like I always did. In the second quarter, I connected with Chris Chambers for 28 yards. That turned out to be one of two passes I'd throw all season, and my longest completion of 2001.

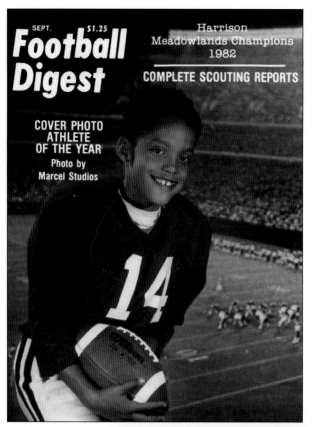

Hey, what can I say—I was born to be a star. Growing up as one of the only black kids in Harrison, New Jersey, sports helped me bridge the gap to everyone else around me. And when it came time for me to choose a college, it was an easy decision: I was staying in Jersey and going to Rutgers.

**RUTGERS UNIVERSITY
BIRTHPLACE OF COLLEGE FOOTBALL**

SCARLET KNIGHTS '94

**CELEBRATING COLLEGE FOOTBALL'S
125th ANNIVERSARY 1869-1994**

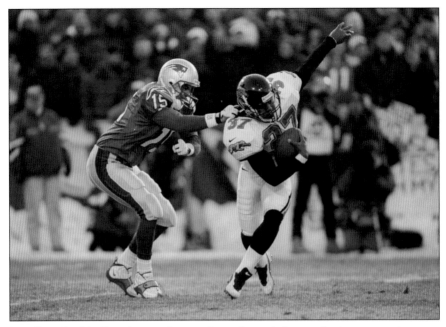

Leading the Big East in passing yards and touchdowns during my senior season wasn't enough to get me drafted as a quarterback; thankfully, Bill Parcells saw something in me and gave me a shot on special teams with the New England Patriots. (Getty Images)

When Parcells became head coach of the New York Jets, he brought me with him. I'll never be able to thank him enough for giving me a shot to live my dream. (Getty Images)

My first NFL start as a quarterback ended with a bad omen for my future—I fractured a bone in my ankle. It was listed as "a high ankle sprain." (Getty Images)

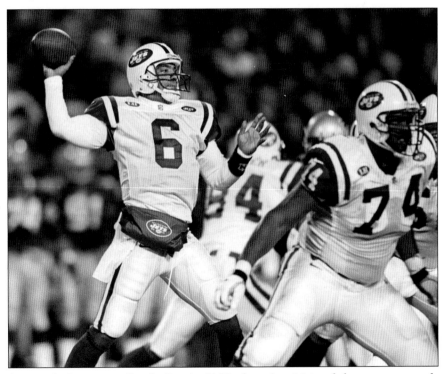

I started nine games for the Jets in 1999, throwing 14 touchdown passes and leading the team to a 6–3 record. I thought I would have a chance to be the starter in 2000. It didn't work out that way. (AP Images)

I signed a three-year, $2.75 million contract with the Miami Dolphins in 2001. The following season, I took this hit from Buffalo's Keith Newman. It proved to be the final play of my NFL career. (AP Images)

My parents, Thomas and Ellen (top); my sister, Alicen, and me (middle); and me and my boys from Jersey (bottom). All of them have always had my back, through thick and thin.

Me and my girls: (clockwise) Cecy, Kayla, Madison, and Rayven.

P.A.S.T. was created by Dr. William Focazio, who remains the driving force behind this incredible collection of doctors and specialists. (Photo courtesy of P.A.S.T.)

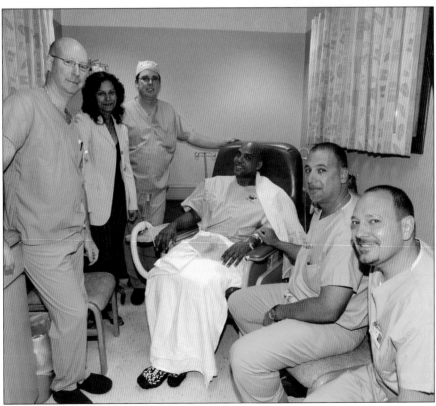

I would not be alive today without the incredible doctors who performed the many surgeries on my back and neck. That's Dr. Sebastian Lattuga sitting to my left, who performed the surgery to repair my spinal stenosis. (Photo courtesy of P.A.S.T.)

Covering the Jets and the NFL for SNY in New York has kept me close to the game I love so much. Even though playing football almost cost me everything, I wouldn't want it any other way. (SportsNet New York)

The next season, I got to experience life in the NFL as a starting quarterback again. But it was nothing like my first go-around with the Jets.

• • •

Despite my best efforts, my back was still in bad shape. During my last two years in New York, I had been taking Toradol injections on game days. If there was the chance that I was going to get in for even one play, I needed the shot. They give it to you right in your ass and it's a full-body blocker. It took care of whatever pain you had, wherever you had it.

Toradol is an anti-inflammatory and a painkiller designed for short-term use. By my second season in Miami, I was taking it every day. I needed it just to get through practice. Even if I was just going to be standing out there on the sideline, I needed a shot. It became as normal a part of my routine as putting on my shoulder pads.

When I was in college, they gave us Motrin. Even when I broke my clavicle, the trainers just sent me home with 800 mg of Motrin. Of course, I followed that up with 64 ounces of Private Stock. That would have normally done the trick, but the pain was so bad I had to call the trainers and get something stronger. They gave me two days' worth of something a little harder than Motrin (no one's giving a college kid more than that), and that was the first time I took any sort of pain medication. Then when I had my rotator cuff surgery, of course, I took pain medicine for that. Pretty standard stuff.

But when I was with the Dolphins, it became an everyday thing. And not just for me. Guys would come in to get their Toradol shots or their Vicodin for the pain or their Ambien so they could sleep. If you remember that Nick Nolte movie, *North Dallas Forty*, that wasn't too far off from my reality.

Nobody thought twice about doing it. It was perfectly normal. It was universal.

By the time an NFL season is a few weeks old, everybody on the field has something wrong with them. An ankle, a knee, a shoulder, a back. You've got something wrong somewhere, so you go in and you take a shot and you go back to work.

We are all just trying to stay on the field. It's not just about winning the game on Sunday. It's about being able to go out on the practice field, which is where you win or lose your job. For most guys, if you can't go during the week, they're not going to go with you on Sundays. And then you're home on the couch.

For 90 percent of the league, that is where the real competition in the NFL is. It's not the games themselves—it's the battle for your roster spot. The battle for your position. The battle for reps in practice. It's not one day a week; it's seven. Everybody sees Sunday, but nobody sees Monday.

I remember one time during two-a-days with the Jets, Richie Anderson had worn out most of the skin on the bottom of his feet. What he had left was blistered so badly, he could barely walk. Did that keep him out of practice? Are you kidding? He never told anybody but Dave Price, who had him soak his feet in Betadine at the end of the day. Parcells walked in one night, took one look at his feet, and asked, "What the hell?" Richie just said, "It's nothing, Coach." Parcells left, and Richie made it through two more practices the next day.

So, I'd get my Toradol shot, no big deal—even though when you think about how many shots I took over so many years, it's a big fucking deal. Nobody considered that there might be repercussions down the road. It certainly never crossed my mind. I was 29 years old. I was one of the best athletes on the planet. I was a quarterback in the National Football League. I was fucking bulletproof.

Until I wasn't.

• • •

The Dolphins were 5–1, tied for the best record in the league. Jay Fiedler led a game-winning drive in the final minute of our Week 6 win over the Broncos with a thumb he'd broken on our previous possession. The thumb on his throwing hand.

The next day, Jay was headed for surgery, and I was headed for a six-week stint as the starting quarterback.

We were playing the Bills at home, and everything started fine. I capped our first drive with a four-yard touchdown pass to Randy McMichael.

We started our next series in Buffalo territory and ran a reverse to James McKnight. I was running toward him, ready to hand him the ball, when I saw his eyes. They looked like saucers because he saw what was coming behind me: Ron Edwards, a 315-pound defensive tackle. He picked me up from behind and smashed me into the ground. I fumbled the ball, but I also knew immediately something wasn't right in my shoulder.

Our next possession ended with an interception inside the red zone. It was the Bills' first interception of the season. But not their last of the day.

Just before the two-minute warning in the first half, Nate Clements got me again. Only this time he returned his interception 29 yards for a touchdown. We went into halftime down 17–10.

In the locker room, the medical staff took pictures of my shoulder. I was sitting with the doctor when Dave Wannstedt, our head coach, came over to check on me.

The doctor told him, "I don't think he can go in the second half."

Wannstedt told him flatly that he needed to get me ready to go, that we didn't have anybody else. The next guy on our depth chart was Sage Rosenfels, a second-year guy we signed over the summer. He'd never played a snap in the NFL.

The doc told Wannstedt he didn't want to shoot me up, that he was worried about the damage I'd already done to my shoulder over the years. Wannstedt left, and I figured, *Well, I guess I'm done for the day.* Doctor's orders.

But then Wannstedt came back. With the trainer. And the needle.

He told me point-blank, "We need you, Ray."

I said, "Okay." What else could I say? I didn't want to come out of the game any more than he wanted me to.

The trainer stuck the needle in, first in the front of my shoulder. He moved it around until he hit the right spot. As soon as I said, "Oooh, right there," he released the juice and everything in that area got warm. Then he moved to another spot in the back of the shoulder, started turning the needle around inside me in an expanding circle until he found the target.

"Oooh."

More juice.

He moved around the shoulder until he'd given me shots in about six places. By the time we came out for the second half, I couldn't feel anything in my shoulder.

On the first possession of the third quarter, Clements got me, again. In the red zone, again. His third pick of the day. He caught as many of my throws that game as McKnight and McMichael, and more than any of my other receivers.

In the fourth quarter, I missed an exchange with Ricky Williams; we lost the fumble. Then, with a minute left, I threw one final interception.

I threw four picks and was part of two lost fumbles, and still we were close enough to have a shot in the fourth quarter. But we lost 23–10, and I was sick about it. I was pissed about the way I played. But I was more pissed at myself for letting my coach make me lose a game for my team. I should have known better. I was too hurt to help my team. I should have been strong enough to say, "I can't go. If I go, it's not going to be good for the team." I couldn't bring myself to think that way. They said, "We need you." I had no choice.

I went out to talk to the media and told the reporters that, for the first time in NFL history, one man was entirely responsible for a loss. It may be a team game, but one guy lost this one for 52 others. "You don't have to look anywhere but me. It was all me. It was inexcusable," I said.

I bounced before I could start crying at the podium. I took the quickest postgame shower of my life and walked straight out of the building. Walked right past Cecy, who was waiting in the corridor; she could tell from the moment she saw me that I was gone. I didn't say a word to anybody. I jumped in my car, left my wife at the stadium, and drove off.

When I finally got home and came through the door, the first thing I heard was, "Daddy!"

My girls didn't care that I had just thrown four interceptions or that I went 13-for-33 or that we lost a game to a divisional rival. To them, all that mattered was that Daddy was home from work.

Some of the "Why me?" shit I'd been steaming about after the game went away. But not all of it. It wouldn't for a long time.

I went into our home office and shut the doors so I could smoke and be alone.

Eventually, Cecy came by to tell me that Norv Turner was on the phone. Norv was in his first season as our offensive coordinator. But I couldn't bring myself to speak to him. He hadn't been in the room with Wannstedt and the trainer. I should've gotten on the phone and told him what had happened. But I was too sick to my stomach over letting him down to take his call.

Then Wannstedt's wife called my wife. She and Dave had heard about how I left the media room, and she wanted to see how I was doing.

The next day, I went back to work. I showed up early so the trainer could look at the hematoma that had overtaken my whole hip, turning my entire side orange and black and yellow. I hadn't shown anybody at halftime when they were focused on my shoulder, and I hadn't stuck around after the game long enough to show it to anyone.

When the trainer saw it on Monday, he went absolutely bonkers.

"When did you get this?"

I told him it happened when Edwards had piledrived me into the turf.

"No way. There is no possible way you could've played with that."

"Well, I did. I played the rest of the game with it."

I never made any excuses for that Buffalo game. I told the media it was probably the worst a quarterback had ever played in the history of the NFL. I took the blame. It's what the quarterback does.

But no one was going to question my toughness. I played through a lot of shit. That's how I grew up. In Harrison, you either fought or you were bait. You might kick my ass one day, but I'm coming back to ring your doorbell the next morning, and we're gonna go again. And we'll go until I've gotten from you what I needed to get from you.

No bruise on my hip was going to take me out of a game. Especially when I'm already playing through back problems and knee problems and new shoulder problems.

I had the chance to prove that again two weeks later when, after a bye, we played Green Bay on *Monday Night Football*.

Late in the second quarter, I attempted to get the ball to Ricky Williams. As soon as I threw it, Vonnie Holliday blew through the left side of our line and put me in the ground. My right elbow hit first, and my shoulder was jarred by the impact. My head snapped forward and then back in an instant. I immediately lay back on the ground and grabbed at my throwing shoulder with my left hand. Something was *seriously* wrong.

Sage Rosenfels had to finish the half for me. I went back to the locker room, where they took X-rays of my neck. I kept yelling at them, "You idiots, it's my shoulder! You should be taking pictures of my shoulder!"

I had no idea at the time, but that hit was the start of a lifetime of neck problems.

Still, I went back out and played the entire second half. I threw two more interceptions—including another pick-six— and I got sacked three times on our last six plays. But I wound up leading the team in rushing that night and scored our only touchdown on a quarterback sneak.

I played better over our next three games—including a loss to Chad Pennington and the Jets. We were 7–4, still in the mix for a playoff spot, when we went to Buffalo on a cold, snowy December day.

We were down 17–14 when we got the ball on our own 48, a little less than three minutes into the second half. Ricky ran the ball on the first play; he was on his way to what would be a Dolphins record 228-yard day.

On 2nd-and-6, I dropped back and delivered a pass with Aaron Schobel bearing down on me. I was just being the mailman, just like Parcells had taught me. Schobel knocked me backward, and the back of my head hit the frozen 40-yard line. Incomplete.

I dropped back to pass again on third down. This time, it was Keith Newman who got me. He hit me from my blind side and clubbed my right arm before I could finish my throwing motion. He knocked the ball loose and knocked me forward into one of my linemen, Todd Wade.

It was a few minutes before I could get up. When I did, I walked slowly off the field, snowflakes swirling around me as five trainers and doctors surrounded me like a detail of bodyguards.

There was just over 11 minutes left in the third quarter.

I would never get back on a football field again.

9

Plastic Garbage Bag

O fficially, I was listed as questionable. That's what the injury report said:

QUESTIONABLE: RAY LUCAS (NECK/SHOULDER)

The Dolphins were getting ready to play the Chicago Bears on *Monday Night Football* without me. Jay Fiedler was ready to return from his broken thumb; he'd actually replaced me for a few series after I had to leave the Week 13 game in Buffalo.

There I was, summed up in five words on a list I shared with nine other guys. At least there were two Hall of Famers on the list: Chicago's Brian Urlacher (QUESTIONABLE: SHOULDER) and Miami's Cris Carter (PROBABLE: KIDNEY). Pretty good company, I guess.

But those five words could not do justice to where I was at that moment. All the papers said, though, was that I had suffered a "stinger." Which doesn't sound so bad, does it?

The truth was I was in agony. After the second Buffalo game, I was suffering from pain in my elbow, my shoulder, and my neck. Then there were my knees, which ached so much I had to soak in the hot tub at night even after getting treatment at the team facility. And, of course, there was my back, with the two herniated discs that were degenerating every day. Sometimes, the pain would be so bad I couldn't get out of my Mercedes. My wife would call me, wondering where I was, and I'd tell her I'd been out in the driveway for the last 40 minutes, trying to get myself out of the car.

QUESTIONABLE: RAY LUCAS (NECK/SHOULDER)

When the season was over, I went to see Dr. James Andrews, the orthopedic surgeon who has worked on about a million professional athletes, about my shoulder and elbow. After the hit in Green Bay, my arm frequently got stuck in a V shape; when it locked, I couldn't bend it or straighten it out. I had to pull on it and push on it one way or the other until it cracked and released.

The doctors in Miami took the original MRI, but I said I wanted a second opinion. And Dr. Andrews was that second opinion.

He was a hysterical guy. We would be in the room with my pictures up on the lightboard, and he'd be surrounded by his team of 15 doctors that follow him everywhere. He'd point to something in the picture, then point to one of his minions and say, "You. What is that? Go."

The doctor would start talking and Andrews would cut him off: "You're an idiot." He'd point to the next one. "You. Go."

I was just sitting there, laughing my ass off, watching Dr. Andrews do his thing. Then he told me what he saw: four bone chips floating around in my elbow. One of them kept getting wedged in the joint and acting like a doorstop. That's why my arm kept locking up on me.

He saw plenty of wear and tear on my shoulder, but he didn't think he needed to go in and do a major procedure. His plan was to fix the elbow, remove the bone fragments, and while he was in there, he'd reach up and clean out as much of the shoulder area as he could.

"I'll keep it nice and clean, and you'll be all right. You want to do it today?"

I said, "Yeah. But I'm leaving tonight. I don't do hospitals."

"I don't give a shit when you leave."

I had the surgery that day, and when I woke up, I was in a gigantic recovery room, with my agent sleeping on the couch and a big fucking tube, like a garden hose, running out of my arm. It was for drainage, which I didn't know at the time. I just looked at the size of it and started to worry that something must have gone wrong,

The nurse came into the room to check on me, and I asked her about the garden hose.

She said, "Oh, that?" And she ripped it right out of my arm.

Lights started flashing in front of my eyes from the pain.

"Are you out of your fucking mind? What'd you do that for?"

"Stop being such a baby."

My agent laughed at me, and then I laughed. And then I left. We flew home that night.

The elbow came back pretty quickly, just like Dr. Andrews had said it would. The shoulder was taking longer than I thought. I figured maybe it would be four weeks, but we were six weeks down the road and it wasn't getting much better.

One day in the early spring, I went to the Dolphins facility to get treatment and work out, as usual. One of the trainers said, "Hey, let's go out and throw." My arm was still in a sling, but I said, "Okay. Let's see how it works."

Before we started throwing, it dawned on me that they were trying to get me on tape. They wanted to see just how far away I was from being able to play, so they had a reason to cut me and get out of the last year of my contract. I put my sling back on and walked straight back into the building.

It wasn't long before Dave Wannstedt asked me to come see him in his office.

Wannstedt was nothing like Parcells. When Parcells wanted something done, he said it, and you did it. Wannstedt loved meeting. He loved to meet before you met so you could meet about the meeting.

He started this particular meeting by telling me how much he appreciated what I did, how he knew that I had played through that whole stretch with a separated shoulder and that I never once complained about anything.

I told him, "I know you are probably looking at bringing in somebody else. All I ask is that you let me get healthy and then let me compete. If I lose and you cut me, I can go home with my head held high." I figured I could live with that.

He looked me right in the eye and told me, "Absolutely, Ray. We at least owe you that."

I went downstairs to the locker room, already starting to plan for another off-season and another training camp of playing for my job. Norv Turner was sitting in front of my locker, waiting for me.

Norv told me the truth: they were about to sign Brian Griese. And that I needed to get released by Miami sooner rather than later so I'd have time to find a job with another team.

It took a few seconds for the news to sink in.

"Wait a minute. I was just upstairs talking to..."

"I know where you where. Why do you think I'm down here now?"

On April 28, 2003, the Dolphins released me. Nobody else wanted me. For the next seven months, I was a former football player.

It sucked.

• • •

In mid-November, the Baltimore Ravens called. Their starting quarterback, Kyle Boller, needed surgery to repair a torn quadriceps muscle. They figured he'd be back for the end of the season and had no plans to put him on injured reserve.

They had Chris Redman and Anthony Wright on the roster. They needed an emergency quarterback, so they called me.

It probably didn't hurt that the team they were scheduled to face next was Miami. I'd have insight into the Dolphins that Baltimore could use, and I'd be happy to share whatever I knew. Happens all the time in the NFL.

When you're vested, as I was as a seven-year veteran, four weeks on someone's roster gets a year added to your pension. I just had to be on the Ravens roster for four weeks and I'd get another year. Boller was expected to be out four weeks. Perfect.

I met with Brian Billick, the Ravens head coach, and Ozzie Newsome, the general manager. They told me they would get me another year but couldn't promise me anything after that.

I smiled and shook their hands.

The whole time I was in Baltimore, I had fun. They had a great coaching staff that started with Billick and included Rex Ryan, the defensive line coach. These guys were all players' coaches. It reminded me so much of being with Parcells.

Football had stopped being fun for me in Miami. But in Baltimore, everything was great.

Everything but my back, of course, which was acting up more frequently. There were days the pain went all the way down to my toes with every step. Taking a deep breath was impossible. Shallow breathing was all I could manage; sometimes, I would get light-headed and damn near pass out just trying to breathe.

Still, I wouldn't go into the training room. I didn't want to give them a reason to see me as anything other than full strength.

I was staying with Dedric Ward, my good friend and teammate in both New York and Miami. He had an ice machine at home, so every night when I got back to the apartment, I would ice everything without anyone knowing—not the trainer, not the team doctor, not Billick, not Ozzie.

For four weeks, I was the third-string quarterback. The backup's backup. I ran scout team in practice, and I didn't even have to carry the clipboard.

Then, standing around the practice field before a trip to Oakland, I sneezed. Just like that, I was on the ground.

I couldn't feel anything below my waist.

The trainers took their time coming out. They figured I was joking. There were a lot of guys on that team with some big personalities—Ray Lewis, Ed Reed, Bart Scott—and I fit right in. Sometimes at practice, while a guy next to me was paying attention to a coach, I'd get down like I was tying my shoes and I'd untie both of his. Stupid shit.

They knew me as a jokester, and they assumed I was joking again.

This time was no joke.

"Luke, stop playing around or we're going to call the ambulance and get the backboard."

"Guys, I'm not playing around."

Everyone got real serious real fast. I was patting myself on my legs and my hips—though I'm not sure why. I was making sure they were still there, I guess. I still couldn't feel them.

Immediately, I started praying. *God, don't do this to me. Not this way. If this happened on the field, in a game, I could live with it. But not like this. Not because of a sneeze.*

Then, my dad's voice popped into my head. Growing up, he always told me, "Walk off the field." If you're hurt, get off the field. If you make it to the sideline and collapse there, fine. Just make sure you walk off the field.

Practice didn't even stop. The coaches just moved the drill a few yards farther away.

Slowly, my legs started to tingle. The feeling started to return. I was out of the woods. But the damage was done. The trainers saw what they saw. They knew when I signed that my back was in bad shape. That was no secret. They hadn't even given me a physical, and they signed me anyway. Maybe they never expected I would have to play.

I took a shower, got dressed, and went home, thinking that if I could get past the 9:00 AM meeting the next morning, I'd be okay. Part of me was thinking that it was all over, that something stupid was going to happen to me if I kept playing football. I remembered what the doctor had warned me when he first broke the news about my back: "You don't want your daughters to have to roll you down the aisle, do you?"

But that other part of me—the part that told me that if Vinny was squatting seven plates, I needed to squat seven plates; the part that said, "Oh yeah? Crank the stim up to 51"—wouldn't let me see or accept reality. As Curtis Martin said, "Your mind takes you places way past where your body limits you to go."

I sat down in the meeting room the next morning as if nothing had happened the day before. With every second that passed, my chances improved. Then, I heard it.

A knock on the window.

The Grim Reaper.

"Bring your playbook," he said.

When I got to Ozzie's office, he was great with me. Straight-up honest.

"Ray, you've become a liability. You can be paralyzed, and I just can't have that happen on my watch."

I had one question I needed him to answer for me.

"Is it because I can't play?"

"Hell, no. You can still friggin' play. I just can't let you play here."

Then he paused and delivered the kill shot.

"You know, Ray, this is something that's going to go out all over the league."

I thanked Ozzie and left. I walked to the locker room for the last time as an NFL player. The equipment guy was waiting for me when I got there. He handed me a black garbage bag. While everyone else was up in meetings, I had to pack up my shit and go. At least the Ravens were cool about it. They said I could take as much gear as I wanted. I took it all.

I called Cecy to tell her I was coming home.

"That's it, baby. I'm done."

I'm sure she was relieved. I was still shocked.

I played in the National Football League for parts of eight seasons. Fifty-five regular season games. Four playoff games. One Super Bowl. Four different teams.

I threw 483 passes for 3,029 yards. Eighteen touchdowns. Seventeen interceptions. One hundred and two rushing attempts. Three hundred ninety-six rushing yards. Four touchdowns.

Wide receiver. Special teams. Backup quarterback. Starting quarterback. Former quarterback.

I gave everything I had for the chance to play quarterback in the NFL. Now, it was over.

The hardest part was yet to come.

10

Wiggling My Toes

When you're in the NFL, you don't play football. You live it. Then, suddenly, you're done playing. What the hell are you supposed to do with your life?

Talk about an addiction. There is no drug you can take that will give you what you get from playing in the NFL. Once you get a taste of that life, of playing the game at that level, of being in the locker room, you're hooked. It gets you in your first practice. You walk out there and look around, and you ask yourself, "Is this for real? Am I really here?" They give you a shirt with The Shield on it. It sits right over your heart; you wear it like a badge of honor.

"I'm in the NFL."

Then, one day, you're not. It happens to every single player who's ever played the game or ever will. Doesn't matter whether you're a Hall of Fame quarterback or the eighth-string wide receiver trying to get his coach to notice him playing gunner on special teams. Eventually, the game is done with you. Then what?

One day, you're That Guy. You walk down the street, and everyone knows who you are. When I went to the Super Bowl with New England in my rookie season, they had a Ray Lucas Day back at my high school. For me. For a guy covering kickoffs. Everyone was wearing red, white, and blue in honor of the Patriots.

Next thing you know, you're retired. Now, you're nobody. The same guy who used to walk across the street to shake your hand and wish you luck now walks right past you, never even looks at you. You are out of sight, out of mind. But you're not, of course. You're still there, trying to figure out your new place in the world.

You're used to walking into places and getting shit for free. When I was in the NFL, I never paid for anything. People always wanted to buy me drinks. I used to get $10,000 in Nike apparel. They'd send me a catalog, and I'd pick out my stuff. I had 80 pairs of Nike sneakers—all white, all fresh. Even when I'd go out wearing sweatpants, I looked like I was somebody. I missed the camaraderie of the locker room and I missed competing. But, damn, I missed my Nike contract. Now I have to pay for sneakers, too?

Of course, I missed the paycheck. But think about it—what was I really taking home? If I made $400,000 in one season, after taxes, I brought home less than $200,000. I know that's still a lot of money. But after Kayla was born in 2002, I had three kids, a wife, and a $4,500 mortgage payment every month. We were always trying to stick to our budget just to get to the next season, when I would start getting my checks again.

People wonder why players put ourselves through all the shit that we do. Why we play through the pain. Why we can't tell the trainers what's really going on, so that we can practice and stay in the lineup and keep our job. Why we risk everything.

Most people think it's because we all make Peyton Manning money. Doesn't matter what tax bracket he's in, Peyton's doing all right. I'm sure his house is paid for. You can't spend the kind of money some of these guys bring home. You're set for life on the interest alone.

So, fans hear someone's making $16 million a year, and they think, "All these guys are millionaires." Not even close. For most of us, that's the fantasy. It's not the reality. There's one Peyton Manning; there are thousands of guys like me.

The average length of an NFL career now is about three and a half years. It was probably closer to two and a half years when I played. And every single guy, wherever he is on the depth chart, thinks the same exact thing:

I am going to play forever.

I was in the league for eight years. And except for my two years in Miami, I never made the kind of money that paid for the nice house, the nice car, the nice clothes. When we had the money, we had a blast. Friends and family would come down to Florida, and we'd show them a good time. Even when I was with the Jets, making far less money, we'd get tickets for people. They always wanted to pay me for them, but come on. "I got it." I wanted to share my good fortune with everyone. The team took the cost of those tickets right out of my paycheck, which may have been decent but certainly was not set-for-life money.

When I retired, we had close to $300,000 in the bank. It was enough to get us started on a new life, and my wife didn't need to go out and get a job. But I knew I'd have to go back to work. Doing something. Someday. But I wasn't ready to think about that just yet. For now, we had enough to live on. I had insurance, paid for by the NFL—though the five-year clock had started to run out on that deal. And I had my family.

What I didn't have was football, and I was struggling with that.

In truth, I already had started to struggle before Baltimore called. When training camp started in the summer of 2003 and I didn't have a spot on somebody's roster, I was in a dark place. I was starting to get angry all the time. Sometimes, I didn't get out of bed for a whole day. I didn't shave.

Then the Ravens called, said they wanted me, and it all got better. Right away. I got up, shaved, took a shower, and got back to doing my thing.

Now, though, I knew it was over. Nobody else was going to be calling, and nobody would've taken my call, if I'd had anyone to try. The depression started creeping back the moment I heard that knock on the meeting room window.

What made it worse was that I knew I could still sling it. I could still play. When Ozzie Newsome tells you that you can still play, you can still play.

I sat around in my bedroom, in the dark, telling myself, "It's not fair." Here I was, a grown-ass man, complaining about fairness like some little kid. I told myself that for weeks and weeks. "It's not fair. It's just not fair." Sometimes, I'd get a flash of clarity and hear myself. I would hear the argument that was going on in my head.

"Are you listening to yourself? How old are you?"

It's not fair.

Between my mood and my back, I was in a bad place. Cecy realized it was time to go home.

Her family was all back in Harrison. They'd been there since her grandfather moved as much of his family as he could to New Jersey from Cuba in May 1971. Cecy was six months old when she came to America with her mother, her mother's parents, and nine of her mother's 12 brothers and sisters. Theirs was the only Hispanic family in town for a long time, the same way I was one of the only black kids in an all-white town. Her mother would go to work in a local factory and come out to find someone had slashed the tires on the car her uncle bought her, or come home to find a brick had been thrown through her window.

By the time we were ready to move back in 2004, Cecy still had a ton of family in Harrison, all her crazy Cuban aunts, uncles, cousins, nieces, and nephews. And her mother. She knew she would need her mother.

Cecy also knew I was sick, or at least she suspected that something was wrong with me beyond my back. She sensed that my depression was a bigger problem than just me always being in a bad mood. She knew she would need help with the kids, especially if she needed to go back to work. She was preparing for the shitstorm that was coming.

We didn't actually want to move back into Harrison, and it was too expensive to go back to Howell. We figured we'd try to be a little smarter about things this time. No more fucking dolphins in the bottom of the pool. We found a place in Jackson, about an hour south of Harrison, down in Ocean County.

Cecy did her usual great job making the house look beautiful, but things with my back were getting progressively worse. I had been on a cycle of having a few good months, followed by a few bad months. Now, every single second of every single minute of every single day, the pain got worse.

I couldn't sleep. Certainly not in my bed. Even if I could've made it up the stairs to the bedroom, I wouldn't have been able to sleep there. My entire life took place on the first floor of our house, mostly in the rocking chair I slept in.

I couldn't stand up straight anymore. I'm 6'4", more than a foot taller than Cecy, but most of the time I was so hunched over because of the pain, I'd be looking her straight in the eye.

Then came the binge eating. Ice cream. Soda. A box of Devil Dogs. A whole box of Entenmann's cookies—Soft Baked—in one sitting. I'd start eating, and when I was done, it looked like there had been 13 starving football players in the room. When I played my final season in Miami, I was 214 pounds, all muscle. Now, less than two years later, I was up to 310.

The only time I felt alive was when I talked about football. I started doing segments for *Cold Pizza* on ESPN, doing some pregame and postgame shows on the radio. But even then, I had trouble being around the game. I took my dad and best friend to a Giants game, and I started shaking and sweating. My father asked me if I was all right.

"No. I'm not all right."

If I could've jumped over the railing and ran out of the stadium, I would have. Instead, I just walked, slowly, out to the parking lot and sat in the car, listening to the game on the radio in the cold. Even when I was working those early games for ESPN, I couldn't watch from my seat. I couldn't bring myself to look out the window of the press box. I had to go watch the game on TV in the media lounge.

There's a phrase people use sometimes about some driving force in their lives: "It's in me but it doesn't define me." But football wasn't just in me. It *did* define me. For so long, the game shaped every life decision I made. Going up the Avenue in my varsity jacket. Hanging with teammates under the Annie Bridge. Practice after school. It shapes who your friends are, where you go to college, where you and your family are going to live.

You can't just walk away from the game. Most of us aren't ready when the time comes. We don't get to decide when we're ready to go. For most of us, it's "Here's your black garbage bag. Beat it."

In the fall of 2005, Fox sent me to be an analyst for NFL Europe games. Before I went to Germany, I heard from Doug Graber, my old Rutgers coach. He had heard about what was going on with my back, and he called to tell me about a doctor he knew from the three seasons he spent as head coach of the Frankfurt Galaxy.

While I was over there, I went to see the German spine specialist who pioneered disc replacement surgery. He wondered why I had come all this way to see him. Not because my back wasn't bad enough—it was—but because he had worked with an American doctor, who lived and worked in the Lehigh Valley, just over the Jersey border.

As it turned out, I already knew of the medical group in Pennsylvania. Dr. Robert Palumbo had helped me with some of the issues I'd had with my shoulder. He worked with Dr. Jeffrey McConnell and recommended I give him a call.

I had been to see a few doctors already. None of those visits went well. One time, I went with my agent to the Hospital for Special Surgery in New York. The first thing the doctor said to me was, "You have to lose weight."

I wasn't at a place in my life where I could take constructive criticism too well. So, I snapped back at him.

"Thanks, Einstein. How the fuck do you expect me to do that when I can't even stand up straight?"

"Stop eating."

That wasn't the answer I was looking for. So, I got up and tried to pick up his desk and dump it over on him. Twenty seconds later, security guards were in the room, and they escorted me out of the hospital. Not a good day for Lukey.

Immediately, I could tell Dr. McConnell was different. He took one look at my back and said, "You're in big trouble."

He wasn't surprised when I told him I had stabbing pains all the way down to my feet, or when I said that it only hurt when I breathed—which was to say always.

By the time I left his office, we had set a date for spinal surgery. In eight months, Dr. McConnell was scheduled to fix the herniated discs that were first hurt more than five years earlier lifting with Vinny Testaverde back in the weight room at Hofstra.

As it turned out, I couldn't wait eight months. I had been losing weight, trying to get my strength back to get ready for the surgery. One day, I had gone upstairs to shower and was coming back down when my legs gave out. They came right out from under me, and I wound up bouncing my way down the flight of stairs.

I called Dr. McConnell and told him what happened. He moved up the date; I would have my surgery in a couple of weeks.

On the day I was scheduled for the surgery I so desperately needed, I never made it past the lobby. It happened when I started to read the waiver they wanted me to sign. I started to think about all the things that could go wrong during the surgery—the anesthesia, the blood transfusion. As much as I needed that surgery, I was not prepared to die for it, so I left.

Basically, I panicked.

I was lucky they were willing to reschedule me for a few days later, and this time my parents came with me. When I read the forms, I started sweating again and my mouth went dry. Luckily, someone came up behind me and gave me the calm-down shot that I needed. Suddenly, everything was okay. I was ready for the surgery.

I woke up in the recovery room and noticed something unfamiliar. I looked down at my toes and began to wiggle them. There was no pain.

Dr. McConnell had implanted a steel plate with four screws and fused the fourth and fifth lumbar vertebrae together. He removed No. 3, which was completely crushed, and replaced it with an artificial disc, a procedure popularized by that German doctor. No longer did I have bone permanently pinching against the nerves in my spinal column.

The pain was gone.

I couldn't believe it. I hadn't felt that way in years. I was wiggling my toes and crying to myself when the nurse came in. She asked me if I was okay.

I could barely choke out my answer. "I don't have any pain in my legs."

Suddenly, she hit the alarm button and sirens started blaring all over the room. The nurse ran and grabbed that tool they use to test whether you have sensations in your limbs, and started ripping it up and down my legs.

"Can you feel this? How about here? Can you feel this?"

"What the fuck are you doing?"

She stopped and looked up at my face. "You said you couldn't feel your legs."

"No, I didn't. I said that I had no pain in my legs."

She shut off the sirens and apologized.

"Can you take me upstairs now?"

"For what?"

"For a heart transplant. You just gave me a fucking heart attack."

The doctors wanted me to stay in the hospital for four days after the surgery. "No way," I told them. "You got two."

They told me that in order to be discharged, I had to be able to get up and walk.

No problem. They'd given me a goal. Exactly what I needed.

I went to my room and started visualizing walking my ass out of that hospital. Because my vertebrae were inverted, the surgeons had to go in through my stomach. What I hadn't realized is that when they do that, they basically have to take your organs and move them to the side while they go to work. They take it all out and then put it all back, and you wind up developing gas pockets.

My wife had delivered our girls through caesarians. She knew all about the gas. She tried to warn me. "Ray, you need to take Tums or Gas-X or something."

"Baby, I'm fine. Leave me alone."

About 10:00 PM, she went back to the hotel, where she was staying with my parents. Maybe 30 seconds later, I started screaming. The pain started inside of me, and I had no idea where it was coming from. And it was moving. All over my body.

I started to panic.

"Somebody do something!"

I had a male nurse, who came in to check on me.

"Luke, what's wrong?"

"It's the gas pockets! Go grab a scalpel and cut me right open, 'cause if you don't, I'm going to do it myself!"

He calmly suggested that perhaps a better option would be for him to help me to the bathroom. He and another guy carried me in and dropped me on the toilet. I swear, I farted for the next 10 minutes straight. It just didn't stop.

Finally, the pain was gone and I was able to call Cecy. I started to describe what I'd gone through since she left, and she interrupted me.

"Gas pockets, right? I told you."

"Baby, you have no idea."

"Oh, yes I do." She told me that when she had one of the girls, gas pockets shot all the way up into her armpits.

That was the one obstacle. Gas pockets. After that, I was clear. I got myself out of the bed and started walking, and they sent me home in two days.

With a prescription for Roxicodone.

11

Spilled Chili

After two days on the Roxies, I felt like Superman. One hundred twenty-five milligrams of narcotic painkillers will do that for you.

The pain was gone. I was back to my old self. I was smiling and sleeping and happy. I even started to think about getting a job somewhere. We had no money coming in, and our savings were dwindling. It was time.

Before the surgery, I had started thinking about pursuing a job in law enforcement. I earned my degree in criminal justice from Rutgers—just like I'd promised my dad—and that was a field I had always wanted to get into. Why not? All the coaches I had in Harrison were cops.

I always thought I'd like to get into some undercover work, maybe even work for the CIA, but Cecy laughed at the prospect of that ever happening. "Sorry, baby. An NFL quarterback can't go undercover."

I had even started looking into becoming a detective in Hudson County. But my back was so jacked up at the time, I could never have made it through the academy. I had a few leads with some other potential opportunities, but I put my search on hold indefinitely. I had no idea if I'd ever be ready.

Now, with my back fixed, my options were wide open again. I was feeling great for the first time in years.

I stopped taking my pills two days after I got home.

That was not a good idea.

I started to feel like shit, as if I had the flu. I got the sweats. I was freezing and shivering. I had diarrhea non-stop and was constantly nauseous.

Cecy came home and found me curled up on the floor, wearing a hoodie and a jacket, trying to get warm. My face was an ash gray. She was scared by what she saw—scared enough that she told me she was going to call an ambulance.

"You call the ambulance, I'm gonna put you in it."

She was overreacting, and I told her that. I was just sick.

"You're not sick. This is worse than that, Raymond."

First, though, she called my father.

My dad got to our house, took one look at me, and started crying. My father, the toughest man that I knew, my rock, was crying over what he saw happening to his son. He knelt down beside me and said, "If something bad happens to you and you die, they're gonna have to put a casket right next to yours and put me in it. Because I'm not going to be able to make it."

Cecy called the doctors, and she and my father explained to them what was happening. Cecy was right. I wasn't sick.

My body was in withdrawal. I had quit taking the Roxicodone cold, and my body couldn't handle it. It's not supposed to. You have to wean your body off a medication like that, even though I'd only been taking it a few days.

The doctors told Cecy to give me two pills right away. I took the medicine, and within 30 minutes, I was up off the floor, good as new. I finished my prescription as directed. No more problems.

I figured that was that.

• • •

For the next couple of years, everything was good. I started working in the city as an account executive at Platinum Maintenance, a company that cleaned metal, stone, and wood in office buildings. When I first interviewed there, Jim Halpin, who would become a good friend of mine, asked me what I considered to be my No. 1 strength, what made me different from other candidates. That was easy.

"I'm battle-tested," I told him. Nobody else he interviewed had been in more trying situations than I had, making decisions that would determine whether we won or lost. Nobody he would meet worked harder than the guy who started on special teams and became a starting quarterback.

I spent two and a half years with Platinum Maintenance, managing the accounts for 50 or 60 of the nearly 400 buildings we had as clients. I handled two of our biggest ones: the Goldman Sachs Tower on West Street and the UBS offices on Park Avenue, a few blocks down from NFL headquarters. When the economy went bad and Goldman Sachs employees started writing things and scratching shit into the walls of the executive elevators, I got the call to get it taken care of.

At the same time, I also started working for SNY, the one cable channel in New York that did a ton of Jets-specific programming. I did two shows during the week and a postgame show on Sundays. I was calling Rutgers games on the radio and doing some spots on ESPN radio. I had found a way to keep football in my life. I was okay with it.

My wife and kids were doing great. We were getting back on our feet financially. Life was moving forward.

Until the spasms started.

They began as minor tremors in my hands. Without warning, my hands would start trembling, often without me even noticing it. One time, my mother spotted me in mid-spasm and asked, "Would you stop doing that?"

"Doing what?"

I couldn't control my hands, shoulders, or neck or stop them from shaking once a tremor started. It probably looked to anyone watching like I had Parkinson's.

The spasms grew more frequent and more severe. They would start in my shoulder blades and travel down my arms. Sometimes, my arms would just shoot out from my sides, away from my body, like I was extending them to have my wingspan measured at the scouting combine.

Then the pain returned. This time, though, it wasn't my back. It was my neck. Specifically, the pain was originating in the area the Dolphins doctors examined during the Green Bay game, when I thought they should be looking at my shoulder.

Things got gradually worse over the course of a few months, so I went to see Dr. McConnell again. The MRI results confirmed what he suspected when I walked in the door: I needed another disc replacement. This time, it was the vertebrae in my neck that were herniated and unstable and pinching on the nerves.

But there was a new problem this time, a complication I hadn't encountered with the back surgery. By this point, I had been out of the NFL for more than five years.

My league-provided insurance coverage had run out.

The NFL covers its former players' health insurance for five years. That was the length of time agreed upon between the league and the NFL Players Association, our union, through multiple collective bargaining agreements. After five years, we're on our own. Most of the time, the five-year clock expires before the time bomb goes off inside of us. A lot of the long-term health issues don't begin to surface until well after we're retired, even though the damage was done while we were playing.

When I lost my NFL health insurance, I was able to purchase my own policy, which ran me about $1,800 a month. That was more than the mortgage payment on our house in Jackson. And that was just to cover me—we couldn't afford the premiums on a policy that would cover Cecy and the girls, too.

No surprise, the new insurance didn't cover any of my pre-existing conditions, which made it pretty much useless in my case. My whole body was a pre-existing condition.

The new policy certainly was not going to cover the untold thousands of dollars it would cost for the surgery I needed to repair and replace the discs damaged in my neck during my football career. I joked with Dr. McConnell about it, wondering if he might let me pay it off over the next 20 years or so.

"Sorry," he joked back. "But we don't take IOUs for neck surgery."

That was my latest dilemma. I knew I needed to have the surgery, but I also knew I couldn't afford it. So, we started to call around to see what kind of help might be out there for someone in my situation. Not an easy step to take for an NFL player, who comes from a culture where any sign of weakness is unwelcome. We're not particularly good at asking for help.

Then we waited.

When I was in the NFL, I never waited for anything. When an NFL player needs something done, it gets done. God forbid I came out of a game with a hangnail—someone would be setting me up to see a specialist the next day. We were always at the front of the line, the first to see the doctor and the first one out. People would do cartwheels and back flips to get you in and out of the office. If you need an MRI, there's no wait. And then the films are sent right away to the doctor, who is waiting to read them as soon as you get back to his office. Sometimes, the films would beat you back there. You didn't even drive yourself to see the doctors; someone from the team drove you.

For ex-players, it's not quite so smooth a process. Nothing is taken care of for you anymore. Make your own appointments. You're at the back of the line, with everybody else. Test results? We'll let you know when they're ready. Good-bye, good luck.

There was one thing, though, that I took with me from Dr. McConnell's office the day I went to see him.

I left with a prescription for Vicodin.

Over time, my pain worsened, the depression deepened, and my damaged neck continued to deteriorate. The spasms kept coming. Sometimes, I'd feel them at the back of my tongue, like it was going to curl up and retreat back into my throat. I would feel the muscles in my neck clenching up like a fist. Spasms would start to erupt in my arms, and I'd have to clench them down to my sides to wait them out.

I started to seclude myself from everyone around me. I lost interest in the family events that I had always loved. I would be up all night, uncomfortable, unable to sleep, then I'd wind up having to sleep during the day to recover. My world was turning inside out.

All the while, my rage was lurking right below the surface. I'd leave work sometimes to grab a drink with friends in the city, nothing bothering me beyond the usual neck pain. I'd be in the bar, in my three-piece suit, having a few drinks, and I would overhear some jerkoff down at the end of the bar talking shit about the Jets. I'd go over and threaten to punch the guy in his face if he kept talking that way.

My boys would tell me, "We're not hanging out with you anymore. Not when you're like this."

"Dude, didn't you hear what he said about the Jets?"

"Who gives a fuck what he said about the Jets? You're acting crazy."

They were afraid that at any moment I was going to hurt somebody. Or worse, somebody was going to hurt me.

"It's not gonna be one guy, Ray. It's gonna be that guy and four of his friends. They're gonna wait for you to come out of the bar, and they're gonna roll your ass up."

I had only one response for my worried friends.

"They better have five friends. Four ain't gonna get it done."

This was my mind-set at the time, all the time. Being angry at the world had become my full-time occupation. The same conquer-the-world mentality that had helped make an undrafted special teams player into a starting quarterback in the NFL had turned on me. Now, I was ready to fight everyone in the world over nothing.

It all stemmed from the pain in my neck. The Vicodin helped initially, but that wasn't enough. In the NFL, one of the first things we do is build up a tolerance for pain. Then, we build up a tolerance to the pain meds. We needed so much more than the typically prescribed amounts to get any relief at all.

I started going to different doctors, getting prescriptions from them for anything they would give me. I had one doctor prescribing me Roxies, another guy writing me a scrip for OxyContin, someone else getting me Percoset. None of the doctors I went to ever talked to each other. And as long as the prescriptions were for different medications, no one at the pharmacy seemed to notice anything.

I was taking about 125 pain pills a month, all prescribed. Then I started seeing doctors about my depression, other doctors about my anxiety, others about my inability to sleep. I got prescriptions for pills from all of them to fix all those problems, too. Just like Vinny once told me—there has to be a reason for everything you put in your body. I had a reason for all of it.

Whatever it takes.

Cecy had no idea what I was doing. Sure, she knew about the pain. She saw my mood darkening. But she just couldn't understand why I'd carry my pills loose in my pocket sometimes, instead of in the bottle, the way everyone else carries their medicine. She had no idea what I was taking or how many I was taking.

No one did. Once, I went back to Dr. McConnell for a follow-up, and as I left, he gave me another prescription for

30 five-milligram Vicodins. I went back upstairs and said, "Doc, what do you want me to do with this? This is three days' worth. I need about a hundred."

Of course, he couldn't give me that many. "What do you want me to do, lose my license?"

Before long, the 125 pain pills I was getting each month from all my various doctors weren't enough. The pills weren't killing the pain fast enough for me anymore, and I was going through the ones I had way too quickly.

So, I had to look for other places to get more pills. I started getting them from dealers on the street, who had endless supplies and no hangups about getting a license revoked.

"Ray, take me out one night, I'll give you a hundred Roxies."

That was the perfect arrangement for me. I'd take out some guys a few nights a week, and I'd score 300 bonus pills to add to the mix.

In a span of about eight months, I was up to 1,400 pills a month. All different kinds of medications, for all my different problems. Every single dime I was making went to buying pills to kill my pain. I was feeding my addiction and bankrupting my family to do it.

What I didn't realize was that I was no longer taking the pills to manage my pain.

To be clear, I was still suffering from pain, but no more than there had been before. But now, my body was craving the drugs. It had become dependent on the chemicals in all the shit I was taking. It would have been impossible to stop, even if I had wanted to.

And I absolutely did not want to. I was a full-blown addict.

I wouldn't have acknowledged that at the time. After all, taking pills for the pain was what we did in the NFL. When you get Toradol shots every day just to practice, you don't see anything wrong about taking as many pills as you needed to get through the day. But there was no doubt about it. I was addicted to the painkillers, only the pills weren't killing the pain; they were killing me.

The more my body cried out, "I want, I want, I want," the more I had to feed it. I had pills everywhere. I stashed them in the pockets of all my jackets, in my car, and in my briefcase. I would even remove the insoles of my shoes and hide a handful of pills underneath them. You know how squirrels bury nuts in the ground all over the place, and how they remember exactly where they put everything? I became a squirrel with all my pills.

The only time that I ever stopped taking them was when I was doing my shows on SNY.

I would stop the day before so I could be clear while I was on the set. Well, maybe not totally clear, but at least I wouldn't be in a complete fog, the way I'd been spending so much of my life. For whatever time I spent on the air, I was as clean and clear as I was capable of being.

I can't really explain it, other than to say when the cameras came on, the pain turned off. It was just like being back in the NFL—the adrenaline starts to flow, the hurt goes away, it's game time. I spent my life playing through pain, and this was no different. I was talking football, and I felt fine when I was doing that.

That didn't stop me from bringing anywhere between 40 and 80 pills with me to the studio, just in case. My partner, Brian Custer, spotted them one day. I carried them in a black leather toiletries bag that I kept with me, and I mistakenly left the bag out and open when I walked away from my desk.

Brian caught a glimpse of all the bottles of pills I had, and when I got back he asked me, "What's the deal with all this?"

I started to explain to him about the kind of pain I was in and had been in for so long.

"Yeah, but why so many?"

I told him that I took this pill for this pain, and this other pill for this other pain, and how this one makes me queasy, so I needed this other pill for the queasiness. They were all in their bottles, with their prescription labels. He had no reason to think there was a problem, even if he did suspect in his gut that something was wrong.

"Dude, that's not normal, is it?"

"Brother, I gotta have it. If you had all this pain, you'd be taking all this shit, too."

When I was up on the SNY set with Brian or Adam Schein, looking out at Sixth Avenue and all the people and the lights of the Radio City Music Hall marquee flashing across the street, there would be no pain. Not until the show started wrapping up. I would hear the producer in my earpiece starting our countdown to off-air: "Clear in 10, 9, 8..."

Reflexively, my shoulders started to hunch up, resuming their familiar tense, locked position.

"5, 4..."

My heart started racing. The pain ramped up from zero to 175 in less than 10 seconds. My neck was on fire again. I needed to get to my pills.

"3, 2, 1. You're clear."

It was like I was on kickoffs again. I'd bolt off the set and race straight to grab my bag, duck into the downstairs bathroom, and down 12 pills at once, without a sip of water—a skill I had long since perfected. Before I left the bathroom, I'd take 10 more, just in case. Maybe 20 more, depending on how bad the pain was when it surged back into my body.

I'd get in my car to drive home, with anywhere between 20 and 40 pain pills now working their magic throughout my system. Sometimes more. Sometimes, there would be a voice in my head, preparing me for any potential contingency.

What if there's traffic? You can't be stuck in traffic if the pain comes back.

Good point. I better take 10 more, just in case.

Exactly.

Not once did it occur to me that something could go disastrously wrong. It never occurred to me that I was getting behind the wheel and driving in New York City, through the Lincoln Tunnel and onto the Jersey Turnpike, after taking dozens of narcotic pills. I didn't think about who I could have hurt or killed. All I thought about was stopping the pain.

You need to put a stop to it. You need to stop it immediately.

I was taking all that medication but still the neck pain remained. And the spasms were getting worse. One day, I was on the train, headed into the city to meet a client for lunch. An old lady was sitting next to me on my left. A spasm came on so suddenly, I didn't have time to brace my body to stop it. My arms shot out to my sides, and I accidentally punched the woman right in the chest.

If I hadn't been dressed in a suit, the transit police probably would have picked me up and arrested me for assault. Instead, I jumped up in a panic and apologized my ass off. I tried to explain to her what was happening to me, but what was I supposed to say when I had no idea what the fuck was going on? I just said, "I'm so sorry. I have a football injury."

At the next stop, I got off the train, walked up the stairs, and called my wife. I told her I was coming home and I wouldn't be going back to work. I couldn't even tell her what had happened, I was crying so damn hard.

I lost my job in the city. Our savings were down to about $3,000. I was further than ever from being able to afford the neck surgery. We were losing everything.

Cecy was doing her best to keep our family together. She made sure the girls were busy with activities, so they had things to focus on other than what was happening to their father. But they knew something was wrong, and Cecy was honest with the girls about how they were going to handle it.

"We're going to cry on the days we need to cry. Then you're going to wipe off your tears, you're going to take a deep breath, and go do whatever you have to do. What's next on the schedule? Let's go."

She was circling the wagons.

Just as she'd done when we moved home from Florida, Cecy decided it was time to sell the Jackson house and move back to Harrison. She knew in her bones something terrible was about to happen, and she went into survival mode. Cecy called a realtor friend to discuss putting our house on the market. The next day, the sign went up.

It was a blessing that we were able to sell it so quickly. But the buyers were ready to move in, which meant we needed to move out. Just a few weeks before Christmas 2009, we moved back to Harrison and into the first apartment we could find. Down by the Newark Bridge.

Cecy went back to work. She took a job at an adoption agency, a job that didn't provide insurance for her or the girls, a job with a salary that barely covered our gas bill every month.

My depression and my addiction were overwhelming at this point. They had become far more destructive than any neck pain I was suffering.

There were five of us living in a one-bedroom apartment, but it was the loneliest I had ever felt. I would go days without getting out of bed. Four days at a time. Seven days at a time.

On those days when I was motivated enough to climb out of bed, I still wouldn't shower. I didn't shave; I couldn't bring myself to look at that disturbing face of the person staring back at me in the mirror. I wanted to punch a hole through that guy I barely recognized as myself.

I wouldn't eat. I shriveled up to a skin-and-bones 168 pounds. People didn't know what to make of this dramatic fluctuation in my weight. Meanwhile, I actually felt good about myself; my suits were big on me, so I figured it was because I had somehow gotten back in shape again. I had no idea that I actually looked like the Crypt Keeper.

By this point, Cecy knew what she was dealing with. Through research and talking to ex-wives of players she knew from our NFL days—they were always ex-wives; none of the couples we knew had made it through something like this together—she came to see clearly that her husband was addicted to painkillers. She saw me being swallowed up by the addiction and kept asking herself, "Where is he in there? This is not Ray."

There was one question she couldn't resolve, the riddle at the core of my problem: how do you get an addict off pain meds if he's still going to be in pain?

Bottom line, I needed to get my neck surgery. And we were never going to be able to afford to pay for it.

Cecy called everyone she could think of for help. She found every file and every piece of paper from every medical procedure I'd had done and called every doctor. She probably called every single extension at the NFL offices, hoping to find someone she could talk to who could point us in the right direction. She spoke to clerks, secretaries, people in the advertising department. She left a lot of unanswered voice mails, and asked everyone she could reach the same question: "Who do I need to talk to?"

She got the same answer from everyone: "I don't know. Hold on."

She started going to my doctors appointments with me, begging the experts to come up with a plan.

She even tried to come up with a system for managing my meds. At one point, we had 29 brown paper bags—one for each bottle of pills—spread across the kitchen counter in our apartment, each with colored Post-its, in a desperate attempt to organize everything.

Take this with food.

Take this at bedtime.

Don't take this with that.

It didn't matter. I wasn't going to follow Cecy's color-coordinated instructions. Prescribed dosages and warning labels mean nothing to an addict. I took what I needed when I needed it. Forty a day, typically. Sometimes 80 a day.

I'd even begun to work street drugs into the rotation. When Cecy was at work and the kids were out of the house, I'd get my hands on something that would actually make me feel normal for a short while. Everything else I was taking was an opiate, a downer, so I'd find something that would give me a momentary lift.

Then I'd realize that my wife would be coming home for lunch, so I'd take 20 more Vikes to bring me back down before she saw me.

For a while, my wife asked people over to the house to talk to me, to try to bring me out of the darkness. To remind me of everything I was missing. She would read me passages from the Bible or quotes from inspirational books. Nothing worked.

Eventually, people stopped coming to the house altogether. It hurt them to see me. They weren't mad at me. They just couldn't look at me anymore.

I had no idea how much of a mess I had become. One night, I came home from my show, arriving in what had become more or less my constant state of medicated fogginess. I stopped to pick up Wendy's for everyone, and I delivered the fast-food bags to the kitchen. As the girls were setting out the food, they noticed I wasn't in the room. Someone found me in the living room. They all ran in and were floored by what they saw.

I was moving in slow motion, trying to feed myself a bowl of chili—only I wasn't holding the chili. Or a spoon. I'd dropped the whole thing in my lap, spilling it all over my suit, the couch, and the carpet. And I hadn't even noticed. I was going through the motions, not realizing that I wasn't actually eating anything. I was in a stupor, lost somewhere between being asleep and awake. Like I was a living ghost.

In a moment of inspiration, Cecy grabbed our video camera and recorded me. She knew she had to capture proof of what I had become or I'd never believe her. Maybe seeing myself in such a state, she reasoned, would be enough to snap me out of it, to begin picking up the pieces of what was left of Ray Lucas.

She recorded me sleepwalking through my phantom meal, then left me passed out on the couch in a puddle of spilled chili. Then she and the girls went into the bedroom, got into the bed together, and the four of them cried themselves to sleep.

I have no idea how many nights they had to do that.

It would've been so easy for Cecy to take the girls and leave me. I gave her every opportunity; at one point, I told her, point-blank, "Get the fuck out. Go. Take the kids and get out."

An addict gets really good at pointing the finger at everybody else. You never quite get the trick of pointing the thumb back at the person who is truly responsible. Instead, you lash out at whoever's left around you.

"It's your fault."

"It's her fault."

"It's his fault."

"Ain't my fault."

Nobody understands you. Nobody has any idea what you're going through.

It probably would have been easier for me if Cecy had left. I could have killed myself without worrying that one of the kids might walk in and find me. But she stayed. Every time I told her to leave, every time I started a fight with her and told her she had no idea what I was dealing with, she just looked me straight in the eye and said the same thing.

"Sickness and health. In sickness and health."

I was more than sick. I was dying. Cecy was watching me kill myself, bit by bit, pill by pill, every day. She must have known how this would end. Her husband was going to die, sooner than he was supposed to. Either from an overdose or a heart attack or by suicide. All because we couldn't afford to fix my injured neck.

At the height of the madness, she finally confronted me.

"Ray, you are going to die. You are gonna die, and I don't know what to do anymore. What am I supposed to do with the girls? What do you want me to tell them? Who do you want me to get to walk Rayven down the aisle? Tell me."

I couldn't manage much of a response.

"I'm trying."

But she wouldn't hear it.

"No, you're not. We have to scream louder. We have to get help."

I thought I knew how I could help her. I went and wrote out what I wanted to happen after I died. I wrote down what suit I wanted to be buried in.

At least, I found out later that's what I'd done. I was in such a fog, I had no idea that I'd responded to my wife begging for me to fight for my own life by handing her my will.

One hundred million vehicles drive across the George Washington Bridge every year. I took it every time I drove home after practicing at the Jets facility on Long Island. I'd take the Cross Island Parkway to the Throgs Neck Bridge to the Cross Bronx Expressway to the GW, the busiest bridge in the world.

I was well acquainted with the George Washington Bridge, but I still felt I probably needed to drive it one more time. I needed to see it with a new set of eyes, not as a commuter looking to get home to his family, but as a man on a very different mission. I needed to find the best place along its mile-long span to drive my truck off the road and into the Hudson River 200 feet below.

That was the basic plan. I just needed to iron out the specifics.

I got in my truck and drove to the bridge, as clear and coherent as I had been in months. I was living in the moment, my endorphins flowing. This was going to work out all right after all.

I crossed over into Manhattan, scanning the possibilities provided by the upper level. All of a sudden, I was at the line of scrimmage, looking over the defense for a weakness one last time. I took note of the little guardrail that separated the pedestrian walkway from the four lanes of eastbound traffic.

This could make things a little tough.

So, I looped around and drove back the other way, heading west to Fort Lee. There's no westbound toll on the George Washington Bridge. Things were looking up already.

The westbound side didn't appear to have any more favorable options. It looked challenging, but not impossible.

Go lower. Go lower.

Good idea. I needed to check the lower level. Once I got back into Jersey, I turned around and did another loop of the bridge. I was really getting into this fact-finding expedition. I was laughing to myself and smiling. I even started to break into a little sweat.

But the lower level was no good—steel support beams in an unbroken pattern of upright triangles all the way across. I couldn't have blasted my truck through those. I checked the lower level on the way back, too, just to be sure. Same deal.

Guess it's going to have to be the upper level.

Guess so. But I needed to do one more lap, just to make sure. I wound up making three consecutive round trips across the George Washington Bridge in a red truck that day, and no one noticed. You would've thought someone would have found this slightly suspicious and pulled my ass over. No one gets so lost that they do three laps around the GW.

But no one stopped me. Must have been my lucky day.

After exiting the upper level for the third and final time, I headed home to Harrison.

I'd planned my work. Soon, it'd be time to work my plan.

I would go on Sunday morning, after Cecy and our three girls left for church. I would drive to the GW, take the upper level approach, get through the tolls and the merge from 12 lanes down to four, pick a lane, and floor it. I knew I would need to pick up a high rate of speed, so that when I made my hard right, probably just beyond the halfway point, I'd have enough momentum to clear the guardrail, the pedestrian lane, and, finally, the outer guardrail. I figured my truck had the weight to carry me up and over, if I was going fast enough. As long as I didn't get caught up by one of the 592 steel suspender ropes that hold the bridge in place, I'd break through.

I figured somebody would see me go over. They'd see a red truck with Jersey tags, maybe even catch a few numbers off my license plate. Someone would be able to figure out who it was and get the news to my family.

I like it. Let's go.

12

The Jelly Donut

That was a Wednesday. While I was out driving around, word had spread about the way I'd ripped into the "Can you call back another time?" woman on the phone. I don't know if the call had been recorded or if she complained to a supervisor, but somehow the news made it through all kinds of channels until it found a doctor who knew me. He called me early the next morning.

"Ray, I need you to do me a favor."

"Anything you need, Doc."

"I need you to call a woman named Jen Smith. Promise me you'll call her before you do anything stupid."

At first, I wouldn't make that promise. I told him I was finished with all the bullshit and the runarounds. But then I gave in and promised him I'd call her, and I hung up. I figured, why not? My plan was in place already, and my countdown clock was ticking.

I wasn't sure what made me make that initial call on Wednesday. Maybe all of Cecy's pleading with me finally broke through. Maybe it was the humiliation of the video she had made me watch, the recording of me trying to eat a bowl of Wendy's chili that wasn't there. I was able to watch about seven seconds of it before I made her turn off the TV.

Maybe there was still something alive inside me that hadn't been put to sleep by the thousands of pain pills and buried under an avalanche of numbing narcotics. Maybe the kid from Harrison had one more fight left in him.

Now, I was going to make this one last call. I'd promised my doctor. Anyway, what did I have to lose? Now that I had my plan, one more person unable to help me wasn't going to make things any worse.

I dialed Jen's number, and when she picked up, I told her what I'd told the other woman the day before.

"I'm going to kill myself."

I started telling her my story. About the injuries. About the depression. About the neck surgery I needed but couldn't pay for. About the 1,400 pills I was taking every month.

She didn't say anything.

Usually, as soon as I started telling someone that I was going to kill myself, they would jump in and interrupt right away. "Wait, what did you just say?" Jen didn't interrupt. She didn't say anything. She just listened.

It had been so long since anybody had listened to me. Cecy was always there, wishing I would talk to her. But I couldn't. I convinced myself that there was no way she could understand what I was going through. Besides, I didn't want to burden her with any more shit than she was already carrying. How could I tell my wife that I took 110 Vicodins in 48 hours, trying to kill myself?

Once I started talking to Jen, I couldn't stop. By the time I was done, there was a puddle on the table in front of me from all of my crying. Trails of snot were running down my chin. Everything came out of me. I had been able to get everything off my chest, everything that I'd been wanting to say, needing to say. And I said it to someone who just listened. For the first time in about three years, I exhaled.

Jen finally spoke.

"Is this your cell number?"

"Yes, it is."

"I have to talk to somebody about taking your case. I'll call you back."

As soon as I heard that, I figured, "Well, that's that. Another dead end. I'll never hear from this one again."

Right before she hung up, Jen said, "I'm going to see if we can help you."

In the deep, dark hole of my addiction and depression, I saw a small ray of hope. Could it be that someone actually might be able to help?

I told Cecy about the call right away. She heard the hint of hopefulness in my voice, something she'd not heard in a long time. My voice had become one low, deep, sad song. Still, her first instinct was to protect me.

"Don't do this to yourself. Don't let yourself go there. How many times before have people told you, 'We're gonna help you. We're gonna find the money for you.' And then nothing? You don't even know who this woman is."

"Babe, she says she's gonna help me."

Cecy didn't want me to get my hopes up only to get them crushed one more time. She knew how fragile I had become, and how I might not be able to handle any more disappointment. She knew she'd lose me to the cave again, maybe for a month this time. Or worse.

She was right. I had no idea who Jen Smith was. I had no idea she had worked for five years with Mike Ditka and Jerry Kramer at Gridiron Greats, trying to bring to light the kinds of problems—medical, psychological, financial— thousands of retired NFL players were struggling with every day, everywhere.

How could I know? We never told our trainers anything when we were hurt during our careers. No one I knew talked about what they were dealing with after retirement. I took it for granted that I was the only ex-NFL player in the world going through anything like this.

How could I know that Jen had started working with a group of doctors in New Jersey—in fucking *New Jersey*—who were providing much-needed medical treatment to a handful of former NFL players? And that they were doing it pro bono?

How could I know that Jen had recently spent 11 days in a hospital in Mississippi at the bedside of Randy Grimes, who played 118 games in nine seasons as a center for the Tampa Bay Buccaneers? That Jen had been with him through his first two weeks in a rehabilitation center as he fought through an addiction to painkillers? Randy had to get clean before he could have the knee replacement surgery he'd needed for more than 10 years. He couldn't have had the surgery first; the toxicity of his blood would have made it impossible for him to survive the level of anesthesia necessary. Even after several weeks of detox, the anesthesiologist struggled to keep Randy under during his surgery.

I didn't know anything about Jen Smith. Least of all whether she actually would call me back. But a few hours later, she did.

"We're going to take your case."

She called with the start of a plan. She was going to fly up from Texas that day. I'd meet her at the Marriott in Lyndhurst the next morning, and we'd take a car service to go meet a doctor at his office in Clifton.

The doctors who would save my life turned out to be just 12 miles up the Garden State Parkway.

• • •

Dr. William Focazio grew up in Paterson, New Jersey. He played high school football. He went on to medical school, became a prominent gastroenterologist, and eventually opened a surgical center in Clifton.

Then he started hearing the stories. They were the same stories everyone was starting to hear about the issues former NFL players, and other professional athletes, were facing in retirement. He started to hear more about all the uninsured players whose bodies were as broke as their bank accounts, guys who couldn't afford to get the medical help they needed. Guys who had turned for help to the only place they could get it—inside a bottle of painkillers.

Guys like me.

The last straw for Dr. Focazio was a segment he saw on an episode of HBO's *Real Sports with Bryant Gumbel* in 2007. The piece told the story of former NFL players who were talking openly about suicide. The players featured in that piece, including three-time All-Pro guard Conrad Dobler, were introduced to the story's producers by Jen Smith and Gridiron Greats.

After hearing stories like Dobler's, Dr. Focazio knew he could no longer sit on the sideline as these casualties piled up around him. He couldn't help but think back to the lessons drilled into him by his parents in Paterson:

"Do the right thing." "Lead by example." "One person can make a big difference."

He had always remembered something he heard Teddy Kennedy say about his late brother, Robert Kennedy. Teddy wanted Bobby to "be remembered simply as a good and decent man, who saw wrong and tried to right it, who saw suffering and tried to heal it, saw war and tried to stop it."

Dr. Focazio had heard enough about the suffering. He decided it was time to try to heal it.

That's how he came to create P.A.S.T.—Pain Alternatives, Solutions, and Treatments. He gathered a team of doctors, based primarily in New Jersey, a collection of medical experts who spanned the full spectrum of specialties. There were cardiologists and radiologists, psychologists and neurologists, orthopedists and spine surgeons. The doctors of P.A.S.T. wouldn't just fix a neck, a concussion, or an addiction. They would commit to treating the entire patient, head to toe, inside and out, whatever he needed. They would work together in a truly integrated approach to medicine, so that they could handle whatever complicated cases were about to come their way.

Like mine.

Shortly after I met Jen at her hotel—a day after I had kept my promise to my doctor and made that call—I was in Dr.

Focazio's office. He immediately began building my case file—which would grow to five inches thick over the next few years.

We started by creating a list of every medication I was taking, every pill I was swallowing at that time.

We started with the prescription painkillers:

> Oxycodone, a narcotic analgesic designed to treat severe pain.
>
> Roxicodone, an instant-release brand of oxycodone.
>
> Percoset, which is 10 mg of oxycodone combined with 650 mg of acetaminophen.

The chances for developing a dependency on any one of these three drugs were considered moderate to high.

Then we added to the list everything else I was taking for the pain:

> Celebrex, a non-steroidal anti-inflammatory to ease the pain of arthritis.
>
> Lidoderm, a patch which contained lidocaine, a local anesthetic.
>
> Duragesic, a patch normally used for chronic pain; it delivers fentanyl, a Schedule II opioid, same as methadone, morphine, and oxycodone. Cocaine is a Schedule II stimulant.
>
> Ketamine, a Schedule III depressant, commonly used as a general anesthetic before surgeries.
>
> Carisoprodol, a Schedule IV muscle relaxant.
>
> Arthrotec, another non-steroidal anti-inflammatory, this one used to treat the stomach issues that are often the side effects of pain medication.

Then there were pills for my depression:

Lexapro

Cymbalta

Plus pills to help me sleep:

Ambien

Lunesta

And there were supplements:

TriFlex, which contained glucosamine chondroitin, used to soothe arthritic joint pain. I was taking chondroitin and glucosamine supplements individually, as well.

GABA, to boost gamma-aminobutyric acid, a neurotransmitter involved in relieving stress. Low GABA levels are thought to contribute to depression.

DHEA, to boost the natural hormone dehydroepiandrosterone, which is produced in the adrenal gland and in the brain to ward off depression.

Tryptophan, an amino acid supplement used to treat sleep issues and anxiety.

Melatonin, used to help regulate sleep cycles.

Magnesium, for the heartburn all this shit gave me.

I could tell by his expression that Dr. Focazio couldn't believe what I'd just told him.

"Are you sure? You're taking *all* of these?"

It was particularly concerning because Dr. Focazio was familiar with the mind of an addict. He knew that you could take whatever an addict admitted to doing and double it to get a more accurate estimate.

He told me what, deep down, I already knew: the combination of medications I was taking—never mind the quantity—was causing more damage than benefit. He explained to me that, for example, either Arthrotec or Celebrex on its own could cause bleeding in the gastrointestinal tract. I was taking both. He knew that the amount of acetaminophen in the Percoset alone could be toxic to the liver.

He knew I was in bad shape.

But he also knew that he couldn't take me off the pain medication without a pain management plan, and without fixing the pain. And that was the P.A.S.T. protocol: find the most pressing problem and address it first.

For me, the immediate plan was to determine what needed to be fixed and in what order, and to manage my medications for the short term.

At some point, I would need to get clean. First, I needed to get fixed.

Dr. Focazio assured me they could help me. I couldn't believe it. There really was help out there for me. There really were people who gave a shit about someone they didn't even know. They knew I used to play in the NFL, but they had no idea who Ray Lucas was. And it didn't matter. They were going to help me.

Doc sent me straight for an electrocardiogram, a test where they stick all these wires to your chest, attach you to a machine, and test the condition of your heart. The technician started reading the printout and froze. He looked up at me, back down at the readout, and ran out of the room. He came back with a doctor who told me I needed to get to the heart specialist in Montclair. Right fucking now.

It turned out my blood pressure was 280 over something. The range for a normal systolic reading is 120 to 125; that's a measurement of the pressure in the arteries when the heart beats. A systolic reading of 140 is considered the start of Stage 1 high blood pressure. Stage 2 starts at 160. I was at 280.

Further tests showed that my heart was double its normal healthy size. I was developing cardiomyopathy, a weakening of the heart muscle, and was on my way to congestive heart failure. It was not a question of if, but when. One of the doctors told me that I should have been dead already.

After hearing that good news, I went back to the P.A.S.T. clinic in Clifton, where I met Dr. Vincent McInerney, an orthopedic surgeon, and Dr. Arash Emami, a spine surgeon. I told Dr. Emami what I'd been told about my neck, that I needed a disc replacement.

The MRI they took that day told him otherwise.

An entire group of doctors came to see me. That was not a good sign.

They told me that disc replacement was no longer an option. Instead, I needed a titanium plate implanted into my neck, fixed into place with several titanium screws, and that a couple of my cervical vertebrae would have to be fused together.

I had a condition called spinal stenosis, which meant that my spinal column was basically collapsing, causing pressure to build on the nerves in my spinal cord. They analogized it to a jelly donut: when you squeeze one, the jelly is forced out and the donut is flattened. The diameter of a normal spinal column is supposed to be 12 millimeters; mine was six.

That can happen to people over time, if they're losing bone mass through osteoporosis. Or it can happen as a result of trauma, a single accident or a football career's worth of them. Had I been able to afford the surgery when my neck issues were first diagnosed a year or so earlier, I could have had the disc replacement. It's still major surgery, but nothing compared to what I was now facing.

I guess it could have been worse. Christian Okoye's neck problems were even more severe than mine. I hadn't met Christian yet; he and I wouldn't hook up until after he too came to P.A.S.T. I only knew of him the way everyone else did—as the bruising running back who played six seasons for the Kansas City Chiefs. In 1989, he led the NFL with 370 carries and 1,480 yards. He was the "Nigerian Nightmare," a 260-pound track star turned running back with big-ass shoulder pads and a neck roll.

I always figured he wore them to intimidate his opponents. It wasn't until I met him that I found out he wore them out of necessity.

Christian hurt his neck in a training camp practice in 1989—before his monster season. The Chiefs were playing Bull in the Ring, the same drill our coaches put us through at Harrison High School. Christian was the bull. He heard a teammate coming from behind and turned to strike first, hitting before he could be hit.

He fell down in the middle of the ring, unconscious and paralyzed for about 25 seconds. When the feeling came back to his body, he got up and left the field. He went through some screening tests, but no one really talked to him about what they'd found. The training staff made a few modifications to his equipment and, soon enough, he was back on the field, running people over. He had no understanding of the extent of his injury. He never thought to ask. In those days, no one did. The NFL wasn't offering up information about the long-term ramifications of the injuries we were suffering, and we never went looking for it.

Sometimes, Christian would hit someone so hard that his shoulder would pop out of its socket. When it did, he'd just reach under his pads, pop it back into place, and keep playing. Christian stayed in the game as long as he could, until injuries to his neck, shoulder, knees, and lower back forced him to retire at the age of 31. Just eight years after he first picked up a football.

Over time, he noticed a steady decline in his strength. He continued to work out after he left the game—walking, jogging, riding his bike, lifting. But he found that he was getting weaker, that he could lift less and less weight as time went by. Soon, he developed issues with his balance. His gait became awkward. If he didn't pay attention to every step he took, he would stagger and, occasionally, fall down. Eventually, he went to a chiropractor, who took one look at him and sent him to another specialist. They scheduled a CAT scan to find out the extent of the damage to Christian's neck. To see what kind of shape his jelly donut was in.

The doctors told Christian that the area around his C4 and C5 vertebrae had been flattened so completely they could barely see his spinal cord in the scan. They immediately set a date for surgery and told him to take every precaution before the procedure; one more fall could leave him paralyzed.

That's pretty much the same thing Dr. Emami told me. He wanted me to be especially cautious driving over the next few months; if someone were to even bump me from behind, I could wind up in a wheelchair for the rest of my life.

Christian had his surgery. Doctors implanted two nine-inch titanium rods, running from the cervical vertebrae in his neck to the thoracic vertebrae in the middle of his back. Sixteen screws secured his spine into the rods, which would hold it in place like titanium scaffolding.

My neck surgery wouldn't be quite as drastic. My steel plate would be only four inches deep, with only eight screws.

By the end of that first day at P.A.S.T., Cecy and I started to believe. We had found the help we needed. We saw that these guys weren't just paying lip service to what they would do for me; they were actually doing it. Already. They were doing tests and getting results and coming up with a plan, all in one day. Just like it used to be when I was in the league.

That night, Cecy got a call from Jen, asking her if they could meet at the hotel. Cecy got there around 9:00 PM and found Jen sitting down, finally, to have dinner. Then she told Cecy what my wife already knew:

"Your husband is a ticking time bomb. If we don't act fast, he's going to die."

Cecy broke down. She wasn't surprised, but hearing someone else confirm her worst fears was overwhelming.

Jen put down her knife and fork, leaned over, and grabbed Cecy's hand.

"Don't worry. We're here for you. We're going to do everything we can do to fix this."

And, true to her word, she did.

I didn't always make it easy on either of them. Once we had set a date for the surgery, I started to get impatient. I was still taking pain meds—in a managed way—but now that the finish line was in sight, I couldn't wait to get there. I would call Jen at all hours of the night—sometimes at 3:00 or 4:00 AM—and ask her, "Can we do the surgery today? How about tomorrow? Is Wednesday good? I'm free Wednesday."

Soon after I met her, Jen arranged for me to visit Dr. Sebastian Lattuga, a spinal surgeon on Long Island whose practice was about 15 minutes from the Hofstra University campus where the Jets used to practice. Like all the doctors associated with P.A.S.T., he would be donating his time pro bono.

I liked Dr. Lattuga right away. He walked me and Cecy through the procedure and explained to us exactly what he was going to do. He said, "I'm going to do the surgery, but God does the healing." He also asked me what kind of music I liked.

Sure enough, on September 15, 2010, I went in to have my neck surgically repaired. And, as I lay there on the operating table, I heard Eminem's voice coming through the speakers in the room. Dr. Lattuga popped his face right into mine, taking up my entire field of vision.

"Are you ready?"

He phrased it like a question, but he wasn't asking. He screamed it in my face, like a wrestler. Or a rock star. Or a football coach.

I started counting backward. In about five seconds, I was out.

When I woke up, my neck had been repaired.

My biggest problem had not.

13

Surrender

On January 26, 1997, the Green Bay Packers beat the New England Patriots in Super Bowl XXXI in New Orleans. I was there, playing special teams for the Patriots. It was the end of my first season in the NFL.

The next time the Packers won the Super Bowl, 14 years and 11 days later, they beat the Pittsburgh Steelers in Dallas. I wasn't there. I was in Florida for my first full day in rehab.

Getting to the Super Bowl was not easy.

Getting me to rehab was a bitch.

As much as I wanted to move on from the part of my life that had been dominated by my addiction to painkillers, I was not interested in going into rehab. I suffered from depression. I had anxiety. I had pain. I could live with all that, with people knowing all that about me. But to add the stigma of going to rehab—of officially declaring to the world that I was an addict—on top of everything else? I wasn't having it.

I didn't tell my wife I wasn't going. To her, it was always, "Sure, baby. Absolutely, baby." Whenever she started to talk about rehab, I played right along with the plan. "Of course, baby, I'm all in. Right after the season. I'm going. I promise."

Only I wasn't going. No fucking way.

It was just like the old concussion check on the sideline.

"You okay?"

"Yeah."

"What day is it?

"Yeah."

This time, it was, "Ray, you are going to rehab."

"Yeah."

"You understand this is for real, right?"

"Yeah."

Yeah, right.

After my neck surgery, I was still in pain. My doctors told me from the start that I would never be pain-free again, that there would always be some measure of discomfort for the rest of my life. But at least this was a manageable pain. I could live and function through this pain.

I was still taking pain pills, but nowhere near to the extent of what I had been before the surgery. Now, I was on a managed regimen, maybe three or four prescription pills per day. A little more on some days, if I felt I needed it. Maybe I'd go off the plan every once in a while, pick up something on the side, a little here, a little there. But it was not nearly the amount I had been doing. And it definitely was not the crazy-ass assortment of meds, where everything I was taking would counteract and complicate and contradict everything else.

The doctors at P.A.S.T. felt this course of action—surgery, followed by a pain management plan, followed by rehab—was the best approach for me. They saw how hard it had been for Randy Grimes, who had to quit his narcotic addiction first so that his body could handle going through a knee replacement, after which they gave him as much pain medication as they were legally allowed to. And then he went back to rehab a second time, as planned, to quit the pills for good.

In my case, they felt that the first priority was getting my neck fixed. Once the source of the pain was gone, we could turn our attention to my addiction. So, during the fall of 2010, I remained on my meds, according to a plan. And I got to keep working.

Again, they felt this was important for me. Covering the Jets for SNY wasn't just good for me psychologically; we needed the paycheck. P.A.S.T. picked up the medical bills, but Cecy and I still had nothing in the bank. We still needed food. I had to work, so the doctors came up with a plan that allowed me to work the 2010 season, under one condition—I had to agree to go to rehab when it was over.

I agreed to do it. Out loud, all the time, to everybody.

But I had no plans of actually going.

Lucky for me, the 2010 football season seemed like it would never end. The Jets had surprised everyone by going to the AFC Championship Game the year before—the first time they'd been that far since that day in the wind in Denver when we fumbled away our Super Bowl trip. In 2009, the Jets had a new coach, Rex Ryan, who was with the Ravens during my few weeks in Baltimore, and a rookie quarterback, Mark Sanchez. Now in their second seasons, the two led the team to 11 wins—the most by a Jets team since 1998, when Vinny was at quarterback and I was mostly carrying a clipboard. The 2010 Jets beat Peyton Manning and the Colts on the road in the wild card round of the playoffs, beat Tom Brady and the Patriots on the road in the divisional round, and were headed to Pittsburgh to play for a trip to Super Bowl XLV.

As long as the Jets kept winning, I still had work to do. *Jets Nation, Jets Game Plan, Jets Post Game Live*—all my shows on SNY. I got to keep working with my guys, Brian Custer, Adam Schein, and Joe Klecko. I got to keep talking Jets football. And I got to keep my ass out of rehab.

When the Jets lost to the Steelers, I lost my only excuse, my get-out-of-jail-free card.

We finished our last show of the season, breaking down the team's loss in Pittsburgh. We wrapped, everyone around the studio congratulated each other for a good year of shows, and I headed to my car (without stopping in the downstairs bathroom).

The minute I stepped outside, my phone rang. It was Cecy.

"Are you ready to go?"

"What are you talking about? Ready to go where?"

"The season's over, Raymond."

"We'll talk about it when I get home."

"It's time."

"Yeah."

"You're going to rehab."

"Yeah."

I got home, and Cecy was ready for me. Her message left little room for negotiation. No wiggle room for Lukey.

"You go or I go."

After all I had put her and the girls through, after all the times I provoked her and even screamed at her to get out, she had reached this point. Either I go to rehab or she and the girls were gone.

We decided that on my way to rehab, I would visit Radio Row in Dallas, where media from all over the country would be gathered to broadcast their shows live on-site during Super Bowl week. And I would share my story with whoever would have me.

At first, I wasn't totally on board with that part of the plan. Jen Smith had asked me how I felt about getting my story out there. She worked so hard to raise awareness of the struggles of retired NFL players, and she believed I had a powerful story to tell. I'd be down there with Randy, putting a face on a problem the NFL hadn't been eager to publicize or even acknowledge. Randy would be the face of the guy in recovery, and I would be the face of the guy going into rehab.

Talking has never been a problem for me. But talking about my ordeal was another story.

When Jen first asked me what I thought about doing interviews up and down Radio Row, my first reaction was, "Are you out of your mind? Do you know where I live? I'm from fucking Jersey. You can't show people weakness here. If they think I'm weak, they'll come knock on my door."

Eventually, it dawned on me that perhaps I had a responsibility to speak up. By that time, I knew I wasn't the only guy going through this. Take Randy, for example. I was taking 1,400 pills a month; he was taking 1,500. The fact that P.A.S.T. even existed showed that there was a greater need out there than I had ever considered.

I talked to Cecy about going to Dallas to tell my story.

"How many more guys are there like me out there?"

"I don't know. But I know you're not the only one."

"This really isn't about me anymore, is it?"

"It is. But it isn't."

I decided to go to Dallas and tell people what I had been through. What I was still going through. What I was about to go through. I would go to Radio Row for four days and tell my story.

Randy would be with me. The year before, Randy had tried to tell his story. People around the league called him a liar. Now, I'd be coming with the same story. Maybe they would listen this time.

That didn't mean I was done looking for ways to get out of going to rehab. I spent my career keeping plays alive once they'd broken down; I wasn't running out of bounds on this argument just yet.

Right before I left, I told Cecy that I wanted to come home after the Super Bowl to say good-bye to the girls.

No deal. She knew that was just an excuse. She knew that if I got on a plane in Dallas bound for New Jersey, they would never get me back on the plane to Florida.

We fought about it almost until the day I left. In the end, I went to Dallas, prepared to tell my story at the Super Bowl, and prepared to go to rehab on Thursday.

Then I couldn't get out of Dallas.

Super Bowl week in February 2011 was a disaster. An ice storm hit Texas and shut everything down in and around the city of Dallas. They had four days of sub-freezing temperatures, which is unheard of down there. Chunks of ice were falling off Cowboys Stadium. The airports were shut, highways were shut, people taking DART trains were getting stranded, and hotels couldn't get people's cars up the frozen ramps of the parking lots. Plus, the taxis went on strike.

Thankfully, I had arrived in Dallas with enough pain pills to get me through Thursday. Jen, Randy, and Dr. Focazio were with me, so I was in good hands. But when we found out we were going to be stuck there until Saturday, even they started to worry.

After what I went through following my back surgery, I knew I wanted no part of detox. The prospect of going through it at a rehab facility was bad enough. But to do it trapped in a hotel room in a frozen city? That would be awful. It could've been deadly.

Jen and Randy worked the phones and found me pharmacists who could fill my prescriptions. They even started calling veterinarians for help.

And, as always, I was able to find a little extra help on the side.

A guy I knew from New York had spotted me making the rounds on Radio Row. He caught up to me on Friday and wanted to make plans to go out that night. I already had landed passes to one VIP Super Bowl party, one that he immediately expressed an interest in going to.

"Tell you what," he said. "If you get me in..."

Just like old times.

I took him to the party, and he hooked me up with 35 Roxies. One hundred milligrams. The really good shit. It was like Christmas Day.

It was the night before I was going into rehab.

Why the hell not?

I took five in the span of about two hours and we hit the party.

The next morning, we flew to Florida. I downed 15 pills in the airport bathroom before we boarded the plane. Randy had done the exact same thing before he went in for his first rehab stint, swallowing 15 in the check-in line.

We landed and hopped in the Cadillac Escalade that had been sent to take us to Behavioral Health of the Palm Beaches. When we were 15 minutes away from the facility, I took care of two last remaining pieces of business.

First, I updated my Facebook page. There truly were no secrets left.

> *I arrived in Fla. Randy tells me not to be nervous but that is impossible. I am in the car on my way to BHOP/Seaside. Nervous about everything, my palms are sweating. This weather will be good for my body. Got a text from my mom, she & my family are relieved I am here. I am on my way to start my life over. Can't believe all the FB responses already. It's a good sign & the support is needed.*

Then, I swallowed the last 15 pain pills I had. The last 15 pain pills I would ever take. I didn't want to go into rehab with a loaded gun. I emptied everything I had. Fifteen final little blue pills, down the chute. I had to get that shit in me before we got there.

I was ready.

We arrived first at the Recovery Center, the main office building where I would attend all my meetings. They started introducing me around to doctors and staff; I couldn't remember a single name they told me. I was pretty loopy when I got there. The Roxies were doing their job.

I do remember being told that everyone I met there was an addict. That would be helpful information later, when I was ready to interact and hear everyone's stories. But at that moment, I didn't give a shit about any one of them.

Then I met Dr. Arthur Rosenblatt. We all sat down in his office—me, Jen, Randy, and Dr. Rosenblatt, who just kept staring at me. It made me uncomfortable to the point where the Jersey in me was up and ready to come out.

"What are you looking at?"

Dr. Rosenblatt smiled.

"I'm waiting."

"Waiting for what?"

"I'm just waiting."

He didn't elaborate. He just kept staring and smiling.

I went outside with Randy to smoke a cigarette. It was either that or choke this fucking guy after my first hour in the building. Randy suggested I try to relax. I'm pretty sure he knew there was no chance I would.

We went back inside, sat down, and, again, Dr. Rosenblatt started in with the staring and the waiting.

Before too long, I started sweating. My stomach started bubbling and hurting.

That is what he had been waiting for.

Suddenly, I had an immediate and urgent need to get to the bathroom. I barely made it before I started throwing up. Sweat was pouring out of me. I started shitting gravy. It was like everything inside me just released at once. When I tried to go back into the office, I could barely walk. I was staggering, leaning over like I was drunk.

The detox had begun.

Finally, Dr. Rosenblatt spoke.

"Okay. Come here, turn around, and pull your pants down."

He gave me a shot in the ass, Suboxone or some kind of medicine to moderate the side effects of withdrawal. Soon enough, the symptoms started to subside. For the time being.

They brought me into a room where I would spend the next few days detoxifying. And suffering. It was more like a small apartment than a hospital room, with a bed and a living room. I could go outside on the back porch and smoke a cigarette if I wanted to. There were cameras everywhere.

I don't remember much about the next two days. I know I watched some of Super Bowl XLV in the lounge area with Jen and David Epstein, a writer from *Sports Illustrated*, but only because she reminded me of it later. I know that I took off all my clothes and went outside for a smoke, but only because the staff told me later that I probably shouldn't be naked on the porch.

All I know is that I was supposed to be in the managed detox process for five days.

I was out in three.

I was then able to move to the condo where I'd be staying for the rest of my rehab. We pulled up to the building, and I smelled the ocean. Which made sense, because it was directly behind my building.

"You mean, the beach is right there?"

"Yes. You'll be able to see it from your room."

Holy shit. I could go to the beach? Rehab just kept getting better and better.

I ran inside and found my room. There was a Posturepedic bed for me to sleep on. We had a chef who cooked all our meals.

Plus, I could go to the beach. Sure, I had to take a urine test immediately when I got back in the building, but at least I was allowed to go outside.

I have always loved the beach. We didn't do a lot of traveling when I was a kid. Instead, my parents would take me and my sister to Sandy Hook, a barrier island in Monmouth County, with the Lower New York Bay on one side and the Atlantic Ocean on the other. Beaches all around.

When we were older, we'd take a trip every summer to Wildwood, down the Jersey Shore, not quite as far south as Cape May. We'd stay at the Jolly Roger Motel, a couple of blocks from the ocean, and my sister and I would take the trolley to the boardwalk. It was heaven.

That was a lifetime ago. Now, I had ocean views and sea air from rehab, not the Jolly Roger. I told myself that if I had to go to rehab, this was the way to do it. Of course, I was only able to be there because P.A.S.T. got me in. Otherwise, it would have cost me about $40,000 a month to be there. It never would have happened.

We did have a few big-money sonnies in the program when I first got there. Doctors, lawyers, CEO types. One dude pulled up in his Rolls Royce Phantom to check himself into rehab. There was an 80-year-old man on his second or third liver. He'd been told he wouldn't be put back on the transplant list after he ruined the first one they gave him; he told them he'd just fly to Switzerland and buy one over there.

It was on Day 3 that I met my therapists. My body was still going through detox; I was still fighting through the sweats and the diarrhea, though they were not nearly as severe. I wasn't much in the mood to participate when we started our group meetings. I was in the room, hearing people talking. But I wasn't listening to anyone.

And I sure as shit wasn't talking.

Not here. I could talk to anyone on Radio Row at the Super Bowl, post updates on my Facebook page, and have writers reporting the story of my rehab as it was happening.

But I wasn't going to tell any of these people in this room anything about myself. That wasn't something this Jersey boy was going to do.

I was still angry, and I clung to that anger as long as I could. Maybe it was because my body was still in chaos. Maybe I was still embarrassed to be in rehab. Maybe it was that anger was the only thing from the last few years of my life that still felt familiar.

I sat in those first few group meetings and was miserable.

We'd go around the room and everyone would have to take a turn talking. I'd clench my entire body when it was my turn.

"Ray, why don't you speak?"

"Fuck you. Pass."

"Ray, wouldn't you like to say something?"

"Fuck you. Pass."

After one of my early group sessions someone on the staff let me know that my angry presence and cursing were intimidating the other people in the room.

"Then don't fucking ask me to speak. Nobody will have any problems."

Within a couple of days, my symptoms had started fading away. My body was getting clear of pain medication for the first time since I started taking those Toradol shots on game days. The fog was starting to clear. The smell of the beach was sweeter than I remembered.

Slowly but surely, I started listening to what people said in our group meetings. The more I listened, the more fascinated I became.

There was a guy who lost $16 million smoking crack and banging hookers. Another guy was an emergency room doctor, who was trained in some sort of Brazilian jiu-jitsu. He drank. One night, he beat up four orderlies. In his own hospital.

The more I listened, the more I realized I could say whatever I wanted in this room. The stories these people were telling were fucking crazy. If all of us were to throw our shit in the middle of the room and I could've switched places with someone else, I'd take my own shit back.

I was in the right place. Eventually I raised my hand.

"I think I'm ready to talk."

Once I started talking, it changed me. Immediately. I started to share what I had done, even though sometimes saying something out loud for the first time shatters you. I went from not saying a word to not shutting the fuck up.

Through talking and listening, I started to realize a few things.

I realized that it wasn't just that I had taken a bunch of pills. It's that I took a bunch of pills and got in the car and drove 90 minutes to our house in Jackson. How many people could I have killed?

I realized that my addiction wasn't an NFL problem. It was a Ray Lucas problem. I didn't start taking drugs because of the NFL. I started taking them because it meant so much to me to keep playing in the NFL, and my body wouldn't have held up without them. The NFL didn't shoot up my shoulder at halftime and send me back in the game; I let it happen.

I realized that some of my strengths were also my weaknesses. The very things that helped me get to the top of the mountain—my work ethic, my toughness, my stubbornness, my unwillingness to lose—were the same things that kept me buried in my hole.

You have a lot of time to think when you're in rehab. It's part of the daily routine, actually. They tell you to go take 15 minutes, sit in the middle of your bed, and reflect. When the fog has lifted, you can see things clearly that you hadn't seen before. It's more than clarity; it's like having X-ray vision.

I started to see, for the first time, what I'd put my family through.

How much money I'd spent.

How we almost lost our house.

How I nearly robbed my kids of their father and my wife of her husband.

I thought about Cecy and our girls, huddled together in bed, crying themselves to sleep.

I thought about the video. That fucking chili.

When the truth floods in on you like that, it can be an unpleasant experience, to say the least. Every day you become clearer, the more miserable you feel about what you had done in the past.

And I had no idea how long I'd be there. I had arrived at rehab without a timetable. I knew from the start that I would be there indefinitely. I wasn't going to leave until I was better. Until I was ready to be the father I wanted to be and the husband I wanted to be. If it took five weeks or five months, I would be there as long as I needed to be there. Whatever it took.

At some point, every addict has to surrender. Which I was entirely unprepared to do.

My counselor asked me one day whether I was ready to surrender.

"No way."

She explained to me that an important step in the recovery process is being able to say, "I surrender." That even if it's just saying words that you don't really mean, you have to say it.

"I'm not fucking saying it."

"You have to."

"Well, then we're at a fucking impasse."

It wasn't that I was *unwilling* to say it; I was *incapable* of doing it. To surrender would have undermined everything I stood for. I had never surrendered in my entire life. Not when they beat up the only black kid in town. Not when I went undrafted by the NFL. Not when Pete Carroll told me I wasn't good enough. Not when I hurt my shoulder or my head or my knees or my back or my neck. I was not built to surrender.

But I wasn't allowed to progress toward my recovery unless I did.

For two straight nights, I laid in my bed, staring at the ceiling, trying to figure out how we were going to make this work.

Then it clicked.

The next time my counselor asked me to surrender, I told her what I'd decided to do.

"I am surrendering the addict."

I wasn't going to surrender myself. But I was fine surrendering that other guy. I just had to hope she would approve my approach to this problem.

She looked at me and said, "Whatever works for you works for me."

I took a major step that day. I surrendered the addict.

The longer I was there, the more comfortable I became. We were all addicts, and we could all relate.

I was the young guy in the group when I first got there, and some of the older guys took me under their wing. We would watch the Miami Heat on TV or just sit out on the porch, smoke cigarettes, and talk. We talked about everything. And I had so many questions. I wanted to understand their addictions. Everybody's story was different, but I was trying to figure out what made all of us the same. It was important to see that there were other grown-ass men out there who were going through what I was. That I wasn't as alone as I once felt.

After I'd been there for about three weeks, I was ready to see Cecy. She flew down to participate in some of the seminars they offered for family members. Before she got there, my therapist, Dr. Lukens, explained to me how it was going to go down.

"When she gets here, you don't say a fucking word. She's got a lot on her mind and a lot in her heart that she needs to get out. And you're going to sit there and pay attention to her and not say a fucking word."

That wasn't going to be easy for me—the not talking part. But I assured him that I was ready to listen.

Dr. Lukens also warned me that what I'd hear would likely hurt. He explained that I had been guarded my whole life. I had lived my life as if I were covered up, protecting the football, bracing for the next hit. In rehab, those walls are knocked down. You're open. You're exposed. You're vulnerable. That's when someone can deliver the kill shot.

Cecy was staying at the hotel down the street. When she opened the door, I saw her face and I just started crying. She had never looked so beautiful to me. It was like seeing her for the first time, all over again.

In a way, it *was* the first time. It was the first time in years I was able to look at her through clear eyes. She looked just like the girl I used to follow around Harrison, whose books I used to knock out of her hands just to get her attention.

We got to spend some quality time together over the four days she was there. She saw me speaking and interacting and listening—doing my part to get better. She cried when she heard me use the word *vulnerable*.

Then she left, and I stayed. To finish the work I had to do.

The group was starting to turn over. Soon, I was the veteran of the group, and I would try to help the newbies. It got to the point that whenever someone new came in, I could tell right away what their problem was. This guy's on crack. That guy's on pills.

I even wound up leading a meeting once, when our counselor was running late. I asked everyone to talk about what most scared them about going home. When it got to be my turn, I was ready with my answer.

"I'm going to be in pain the rest of my life. That's what scares me the most. It is always going to be there."

Eventually, I was ready for Dr. Lukens' special group. It was more extreme than I was used to—it met for the entire day, for five days in a row. Doc warned me that the group wasn't for everyone; you had to volunteer to participate.

"You're up there in front of everybody, and they really go at you. They're going to ask you questions that you don't want to answer."

To me, it sounded perfect. Exactly what I needed. What I was ready for. I had to be in that group.

Let's go.

There was a lot of crying in this group, a lot more than usual. Even when you weren't the one in the crosshairs, you were crying. There was a lot more yelling, too. We talked about the underlying factors behind our addictions. We broke everybody down to their nuts and bolts, digging down to the things we lived through when we were younger that we never thought were relevant to anything. People would be talking about watching their father beat their mother, about being molested. And I'd be listening, sucking snot. It was amazing and exhausting and powerful and heartbreaking. And when I was done with that group, I decided it was time for me to go.

Whenever one of us left rehab, we'd have a big dinner to celebrate. Everybody would come to the condo and say something about the person. Then they give you a coin—the Sobriety Coin—and you take that home with you.

Just 42 days after Jen and Randy delivered me to the Recovery Center building, 42 days after Dr. Rosenblatt stared at me until the last 15 Roxies had worked their way out of my system, they returned to pick me up.

I was clean. I was clear. I had my coin. I had my life back.

I was going home to my family.

14

Clarity

I hadn't been home more than a few days before I saw Cecy cry.

We were sitting on opposite ends of the island counter in our kitchen, just having coffee together and talking, when she started to cry.

Immediately, I got defensive.

"What'd I do?"

I couldn't think of anything I'd done. I hadn't even left the house that day. What could I possibly have done to bring my wife to tears?

"We just had a conversation."

As soon as she said it, I understood. We hadn't had a conversation in three years. I hadn't listened to her in years. No "How was your day?" No "How's work?" No "Is there anything I can do to help out around the house?" Nothing. When I was sick, she would try talking to me, and I would either say "Not now" or just tune her out completely. Imagine that—being married to someone who couldn't even carry on a basic conversation with you. For three years.

In rehab, I realized that I'm not the strongest person in my home. Not physically, not mentally, not emotionally. The woman sitting across the kitchen from me that day is the strongest person I have ever met. I've gone to battle with some big, strong guys, with and against the best athletes on the planet. But the toughest sumbitch I've ever known is my wife. Real toughness is not about how much weight you can lift; it's not about getting hit and getting up from the bottom of the pile. That's not strength. That's not courage. My wife may look like an angel, but she is not someone to be fucked with.

She stayed. Most wives don't. When I got home after 42 days in rehab, my wife and my daughters were still there, waiting for me.

Now, my wife was crying because she was happy that we just had a conversation. Moments like that will always make me wonder just how fucked up I really was.

I think God blessed me with amnesia, because there's a lot I don't remember from my drug-abusing days. My daughters will tell me stories about things I did or said, and I can't remember any of it.

"Get out of here. No way I did that."

"No, Dad, you did. For real."

Those conversations upset me almost more than anything. Every day, I look at my kids, and for a moment, I have to ask myself, "Did I fuck them up?"

My kids are terrific. I know all parents think that about their kids, but mine really are something special. All three of them light up any room they walk into. Rayven's the athlete, and she's a bit of a homebody, too. It amazes me that despite everything she's witnessed, she still loves being home. Madison is an old soul; she's definitely been here before. She's a confident, self-assured young woman, and she also likes her space—just like her daddy. She doesn't need to surround herself with 15 people; she's happy going upstairs to her room to write her music. And Kayla is a mixture of all of us. She's an actress, just like Cecy was growing up.

When I got home from rehab, I saw a character trait in Kayla that made me a little nervous, a trait that she and I share: Kayla doesn't like to lose. She takes losing personally. We would be playing cards and she'd lose a hand; next thing you know, the cards were all over the room.

"What's the matter with you?"

"I hate losing."

"Guess what, Mama. It's a part of life."

"I don't care. I hate it."

That sounded a little too familiar, and it worried me. That same absolute hatred of losing is part of what got me out of Harrison, what kept me from becoming one of those Harrison Has-Beens I heard about growing up, guys whose best days were back in Pop Warner or Little League or high school. I wound up starting at quarterback on *Monday Night Football* in no small part because of that refuse-to-lose attitude. That's where it started for me.

Just how much that played into my addiction was something I had to consider during those group sessions in rehab. I spent my career doing whatever I needed to do to win a game or keep my job. Need to get stronger? Lift more weight. Need to heal faster? Crank up the stim. Need to beat the pain? Take more pills. I simply wasn't going to lose, and I almost killed myself in the process.

That's the kind of shit you think about when you get clear.

• • •

For the most part, everything was better after rehab. Music sounded better. Movies were better. Watching basketball was better. To be able to laugh again, even to cry clean, was all better. I felt alive again. But when you have clarity and think about all the things you did and the people you hurt, it can just gut you sometimes.

Something else started to happen once the fog lifted, something I wasn't expecting.

My knees started hurting again.

I hadn't done anything to damage my knees since I left the game. But here I was, more than seven years removed from playing football, and all of a sudden my knees were killing me. Just like old times.

Then I realized they'd been hurting all along. I just didn't notice it because I spent three years on pills.

The pain in my neck was the reason I started taking the pills, but the pills were also taking care of all the other parts of my body that were hurting, without me even noticing. I had my back fixed and my neck fixed, and I went to rehab to get off the painkillers. But now, every football injury I ever had returned to pile up on me. I'd wake up one morning and notice my elbow was hurting again. Or my shoulder was hurting again. My Achilles was hurting. Or my knees. I'd be walking down the street, and all of a sudden I would feel a blast of pain in my knee, like someone had just whacked it with a sledgehammer.

So there I was, home from rehab, clean and clear, but still in pain. Just like the doctors told me I would be.

It turned out there was a bone chip loose in my kneecap, pressing against where the tendon is connected. Ten days after I got home from rehab, I needed an arthroscopic procedure on my knee—something I hadn't even noticed for three years was a problem.

The pills masked more than just the pain from my neck injury. They'd hidden everything.

The challenge for the doctors from P.A.S.T. was not cleaning out the knee. The procedure was basically a tune-up. The tricky part was how to perform the surgery without giving me pills for the pain afterward. Because I wasn't going to take them.

I was not opening that door again. If knew that if I opened it, I'd never be able to get it closed. I told my doctors, "I won't come back from it this time. I'd just go off down the road and you won't hear from me again."

My doctors came up with a plan to use a nerve block to manage the pain. Basically, they injected a local anesthetic in an area that numbs the nerves around the site of the surgery. It could last for a day or two, and if I could get past the first 48 hours post-op, the pain would begin to ease significantly. Knowing the high tolerance for pain I had in the first place, they felt I could make it through those two most painful days.

There was only one problem. To block the nerves in my knee, they needed to do the injection right next to my nut sack.

Like most guys, I'm not a fan of needles anywhere near my nut sack. And when they told me that was the plan, I said, in all seriousness, "You can just wheel me out right now. I am not doing it. I'll limp around the rest of my life if I have to."

But they promised to give me the old calm-down shot first, and that made everything better. I was able to have the scope done without pain meds during my recovery.

I followed the same plan after two more knee surgeries that followed over the next two years. One of those was a microfracture surgery, where they drill holes in the bone with an awl so that blood and bone marrow oozes out of the holes. That would generate growth in the damaged cartilage, which basically repairs itself. The scope was not a big deal. Drilling holes in a bone in my knee? Big fucking deal.

I handled all the procedures with the nerve blocks. I didn't take so much as a single Alleve in recovering from any of them.

But it wasn't just my knees that were proving to be a problem.

A few months after I finished rehab and not too long after the first knee scope, I lost feeling in my fingers. Not all of them. Just the outside two, on both hands. But there was no pain, so I didn't tell anyone. It never even crossed my mind to talk to someone about it. After what I'd been through, I figured, who gives a shit if I can't feel a couple of fingers? It wasn't keeping me from buttoning my shirt or anything. I kept it to myself. Old habits die hard.

I went to see Dr. Emami for a checkup, and he asked how I'd been feeling. I told him about the fingers.

He wound up having to go back into my neck to drill three holes in my vertebrae. The plate they'd put in was pinching a nerve.

Eight months later, the same thing happened. Except this time I lost feeling in my right arm. The whole thing went numb.

I was starting to get pretty frustrated over the issues that kept coming back. We had a meeting with the doctors, where I told everyone I was tired of going through this every few months. Jen was at that meeting; I think she was worried I would snap someone's head off. My ears were red, which is a dead giveaway to the people that know me well. My ears get red when my blood pressure goes up. Bad things happen when Lukey's ears get red.

Dr. Focazio understood my frustration. But he helped me understand that this was not the end of the world.

"Ray, if it were something we couldn't fix, that would be a tragedy. Then, I can see you getting upset. This is fixable."

Dr. Focazio was right. My body had been wrecked over my years of playing football, but I didn't have cancer or something that couldn't be fixed. That made me one of the lucky ones, I guess.

I had seen with my own eyes how bad things can get on a football field. I was at the New Meadowlands Stadium, calling the Rutgers-Army game on October 16, 2010.

The day Eric LeGrand was paralyzed.

Chris Carlin and I were doing the game for the Rutgers Radio Network. Rutgers had scored with 5:16 left in the fourth quarter, tying the score at 17–17. Eric, a junior defensive tackle, was on the kickoff coverage team. He was the first one to make contact with Army's returner, smashing into him to make the tackle at the 25-yard line.

I could hear the impact all the way up in the press box. I could feel it in my chest.

I knew Eric was hurt right away. I said so on the air, immediately. Three times.

"He's hurt. He's hurt. He's hurt, Chris."

I took my headset off and watched through my binoculars as Rutgers coach Greg Schiano ran onto the field. Eric was on his back, his arms and legs stuck six inches off the ground.

And he wasn't moving.

Eric was carted off the field and taken to the hospital for emergency surgery. After the game, Jason Baum, the senior associate AD at Rutgers, called to tell me that Eric had fractured his C3 and C4 vertebrae.

"It's not good, Ray," he said. "They think he's paralyzed."

I lost it. I hung up the phone and could not catch my breath. By the time I got home, I was hysterical, crying to Cecy on the couch.

After seeing Eric on the ground, after seeing the team send for his mother, after hearing the news that this amazing young man had been paralyzed, it hit me.

For the first time, I understood that it could have been me.

Way back when the doctors gave me my two choices—to quit football or to keep playing knowing that, if I got hit hard enough, I risked getting paralyzed—I made my decision in an instant: "I'm playing." End of story. I never gave it a second thought. Not once.

Not until what happened to Eric. When he was playing on special teams. For Rutgers. Both positions I had once found myself in.

In the weeks that followed, I tried to go see Eric. Three times I drove to the hospital and couldn't get out of my car. I just turned around in the parking lot and drove off; I couldn't bring myself to go in.

So, when Dr. Focazio reminded me that my latest problem was "fixable," I cooled off and asked them to make sure that when they opened me up this time, they address any other potential issues. I wanted this to be my last surgery.

They promised. Then they went in and drilled four more holes.

They have not been back in since.

And, of course, I made it through it all—three knee surgeries and two neck surgeries since the end of rehab—without a single pain pill.

I'm clean; I get to feel it all.

Which also makes the celebrations that much sweeter.

While I was recovering from my first knee surgery post-rehab, I got a text with some good news. I'd been splashed out on the couch—the same couch I was on when Cecy videotaped me, spaced out in a pool of chili—when my phone buzzed with a text message from Steve Overmyer, a sports anchor from the CBS affiliate in New York.

It said, "You won."

The text didn't make sense at first. What did I win? I didn't play the lottery that day.

Then it hit me. The regional Emmy awards were being presented at a ceremony in the city. I couldn't make it; I would've needed my wife to go with me, since I was still struggling to get around after the surgery.

I knew I had been nominated, but I hadn't been paying too much attention to the process. There was plenty for me to focus on already, like healing from my surgery and rebuilding my life. On the day I got the news, I'd been back exactly two weeks.

When I realized why Steve had congratulated me, I jumped up off the couch...and then I crumbled straight to the ground. I'd forgotten my knee wasn't ready yet for walking, let alone a spontaneous celebration. So, I crawled across the floor and dragged myself up a flight of stairs and started banging on the door to the bathroom, where Cecy was taking a shower.

She heard the banging, and she must have feared the worst, which I can understand in hindsight. I guess I conditioned her to expect bad news over the years.

"What are you doing?"

"I won!"

"You won what?"

"I won an Emmy!"

She screamed. I screamed. It was just what the doctor ordered at that time. It was a validation. I don't know how big a deal it really is—a New York Emmy Award in the category for On-Camera Talent: Sports Analyst. But, man, it was a big freaking deal to me. It was a sign, like the dolphins in the pool in Florida. Things were headed in the right direction.

And, for a change, the good news just kept coming. Later that month, HBO aired a segment on *Real Sports*, a story by Armen Keteyian featuring Dr. William Focazio; the work being done by him and other doctors at Pain Alternatives, Solutions, and Treatment; and a certain broken-down quarterback from New Jersey who had planned on driving himself off the George Washington Bridge.

It was an emotional night. My family and I watched the show debut at Dr. Focazio's house. It was the first time my daughters heard me speaking so bluntly about killing myself. We all cried together while the segment aired, Doc—the "G.I. guy from New Jersey," as Armen called him—and the man whose body and life he had put back together, piece by piece.

Cecy and I remained convinced that I needed to help spread the word about P.A.S.T. and the challenges former players were facing. We always talked to our girls about the importance of doing the right thing. Same thing Dr. Focazio's parents told him. I had a voice, and the right thing for me to do was use it.

People needed to hear about what I'd lived through. What my family lived through, and that we were still together. Football players needed to hear it, but so did other people. Addiction is not exclusive to football players. Addiction doesn't care if you're young or old, black or white, rich or poor. It just wants to beat you down, put you in a hole, and bury you.

I wanted people to see that battling addiction was not a hopeless endeavor. Which is why I spent Father's Day 2011— my first clean and clear Father's Day in years—at The Life Christian Church in West Orange.

I wasn't always big on going to church. I grew up Catholic, and I did some Bible study with teammates in the NFL. But it didn't really stick with me.

That doesn't mean religion didn't work for some people. It worked for Joe Klecko, my colleague at SNY and one of the greatest New York Jets of all time. One of the toughest football players ever, period. He set an unofficial NFL record with 20.5 sacks in 1981, is one of only two guys to make the Pro Bowl at three different positions, and absolutely deserves to be in the Hall of Fame.

Klecko had his share of injuries during his 12-year career. In the second game of the 1982 season, he ruptured the patella tendon in his right knee; it tore clean off the bone when Joe planted his foot to take on a block from Patriots tight end Don Hasselbeck. It was an injury players didn't come back from in those days. Klecko got himself back in time for the playoffs.

Joe did everything he was supposed to do. He even prepared to begin a business career once his playing days were done. But even having a plan didn't make life after the NFL any easier.

Within a couple of years, Joe lost his business. He lost his house. Then he found God, and that gave Joe Klecko the strength to do what he'd always done: pick himself up, work his ass off, and build his life back.

Cecy also found church to be a place she could turn to during some of our darkest hours. Back then, she kept asking me to go with her to this place in Jackson, but I resisted. Finally, I agreed to go, once. But I said I wanted to sit in the back where nobody would notice me. She assured me that wouldn't be a problem.

We got there, sat in the back, and not 10 minutes into the service, the preacher called out, "Ray Lucas, come on down front." I was not happy. We left when the service was done, and I had no plans to give that church or religion another chance. Jersey boys don't give a lot of second chances.

But around the time I was preparing to go to rehab, I met Pastor Terry Smith of TLCC. He invited me to come to services one day. Cecy promised me it would be different than the last time, that they had real music—even a big band sometimes, instead of using a tape recorder like the place in Jackson.

I agreed to give it one more shot. I'd go one more time, and if it wasn't for me, I was never, ever going back.

We sat through that first sermon, listening to Pastor Smith, and I didn't say a word. We were walking out to the car, and I still hadn't spoken. Not until Cecy asked, "Are you all right?"

"Did you do that?"

"Do what?"

"Did you tell him to say all that stuff for my benefit? To do that whole sermon because I was going to be there?"

She hadn't, which confused me, because I was certain he was talking straight to me. I was blown away when I learned that the whole thing hadn't been staged.

A few months later, on Father's Day, Pastor wanted to change things up. Rather than deliver a traditional sermon, he decided to present a lesson about fathers in a different way. The story he wanted to share with his congregation on Father's Day was mine.

He brought out a couple of chairs and a small table, and arranged a sort of talk show set on the stage. And he brought in Roman Oben to interview me.

Roman and I had known each other for a long time. We played against each other in the NFL. We debated each other as panelists on an SNY show called *The Wheelhouse*; he always took the Giants' side of things, and I always took the Jets'. If nothing else, he and I would make for a lively conversation.

Like most players, Roman racked up a long list of injuries during his 12 seasons playing offensive tackle. As he told the congregation that day, he'd had nine knee surgeries and two foot reconstructions. He spent about two years of his life on crutches.

When I talked about needing to get clean and healthy so I could walk my girls down the aisle, Roman could relate. He just wanted to be pain-free so he could coach his boys' soccer team.

Roman and I talked for about 20 minutes, about everything. We did three sessions that day. It was the first time I'd told my story to a live audience. Radio Row and *Real Sports* was one thing. I hadn't yet opened up in front of a crowd about my injuries, about the pills, about going to rehab.

Just as Cecy cried that first time we shared a conversation, she couldn't help but cry in church that day. Months earlier, she couldn't be sure that I would live to see another Father's Day.

So many people approached me after the services to thank me. I couldn't believe how many people in one day told me that they had a brother who was an addict, an uncle who was an addict, a husband or a daughter or a sister-in-law.

That's why I needed to speak out. That's why I keep speaking out.

• • •

Addiction is one of those things that never goes away, not really. Not for addicts. Not for me.

Sometimes, when my knee is really bothering me, when winter gets particularly brutal or it's going to rain (I can tell you a week ahead of time), I hear that whisper in my ear again.

Take a couple of pills. You need it.

My pain never goes away. Neither does my addiction.

One will get it done. It'll make you feel better.

I'm not afraid of guns. I'm not afraid of getting stabbed. I'm not afraid of any man.

The only thing I fear is one tiny pill.

Because I could never take one pill. It's like the alcoholic who says, "I can have one beer. It'll be okay." Wrong. You can't have one drink. You wind up having 37 of them. I couldn't take one pill. It'd be over for me. I'd be in the dirt.

But you haven't taken anything in three years. It can't hurt you.

Addiction is a cunning disease. It is always there, in the shadows, doing pushups and situps, getting cock diesel.

Well, bitch, so am I.

I'm ready this time. I'm more educated about addiction, about depression, about anxiety. I have doctors to turn to when something's wrong, who can fix whatever is broken or help me deal with the chronic pain I'll never be rid of.

I see Dr. Rish Patel, the pain management director for P.A.S.T., regularly. He gives me pressure point injections to ease the constant spasms I still have in my back, which stretch from my trapezius to the bottom of my rib cage. I have them every day. On the really bad days, I get knots like speed bumps all over my back. Dr. Patel sticks four-inch needles into my back and shoots steroids and muscle relaxants to give me some relief. The relief is immediate but only temporary.

Every Thursday, I get a massage. It's difficult for me to find someone strong enough to beat me up the way I need, but I have found one masseuse, Dana Hoffman, who is sweating by the time she's done with me. She digs in with her elbows; sometimes, it feels like she's jumping off a table and landing knees-first in my back. Which is fine. It doesn't work otherwise. And if I miss a week, my body is in big trouble until I can get my ass back on the table.

I still go to the gym, though it's a pretty pathetic sight. There are kids in there half my size benching 225 pounds. I'm doing a buck thirty-five. It's hard to keep my competitive juices from flowing. I start thinking about lifting with Vinny Testaverde, about what we used to do, and I get the impulse to do more. I feel like I need to show these guys in the gym what I can do. But I can't do it anymore. I'm not allowed to.

I can't lift with my legs at all. No squats, no hang cleans, no leg extensions.

It's frustrating. Sometimes, it's downright embarrassing when I think of what my body used to be able to do. There's no running anymore. If I run on the treadmill, I'm in bed for four days. There's no playing basketball anymore. I help coach the varsity girls' basketball team at Harrison High School, but even just standing up for an entire practice ties up my back.

I just have to do whatever I can to keep in shape, to stay healthy for the fights that are still ahead of me. We all do; we never stop competing. That part of being a football player doesn't go away just because the game or my career ends. A few years ago, Vinny had surgery on his shoulder. It was such a mess that doctors told him it would take five to seven months before he'd be able to pick up a golf club. He was back on the course in three.

It helps to have a goal. I've got mine: I can't let my addiction beat me again. It already beat me once.

This is one battle I simply cannot lose.

15

We Are Not Alone

I was 13 days into rehab when I met Drew Macfarlan.

Jen Smith called to tell me she was bringing someone to Florida who needed my help. It was Jen who brought Randy Grimes to P.A.S.T.; his was one of the worst cases in a pile of files that stacked up during Jen's time at Gridiron Greats, a collection of retired NFL players who needed help they could not find or afford. It was Jen who took my call and brought me to P.A.S.T. Now, she was bringing in Drew, who played football for Duke in the early 1990s, and she needed to convince him he needed to go to rehab and get clean.

She wanted to know if I would participate in an intervention.

I had no idea whether I was ready to help. I had only just started to take the wall down in my own group sessions at Behavioral Health of the Palm Beaches. I was just learning to sort out my own shit. Would I really be able to help someone else? And would it have a negative effect on my own progress?

Drew was a disaster. He was taking pills and drinking half a gallon of alcohol a day. When Dr. Focazio first met him, Drew's gait was so unsteady and his body so dysfunctional, Doc thought maybe Drew was suffering from cerebral palsy.

Jen wanted to get him to Florida to meet with a group of us—former football players, recovering addicts all.

Craig Sauer was part of that group. Craig played linebacker for five NFL seasons—four with Atlanta, one with Minnesota. Countless concussions made a mess of him. On the day that Jen first took me to meet the doctors at P.A.S.T., Craig was in Dr. McInerney's office, talking non-stop. To be honest, it scared the crap out of me; is that what I was going to be like one day? Craig lost his family. He had suffered such severe memory loss he couldn't live by himself. He needed someone to put Post-it notes on the door to remind him if it was okay for him to go outside, Post-its on his food so he knew what he could or couldn't eat.

Lincoln Coleman was also part of that group. Coleman spent two seasons with the Cowboys, backing up Emmitt Smith during the 1993 and 1994 seasons. He rushed for 57 yards in his first NFL game—an icy Thanksgiving Day in Dallas that Leon Lett would like to forget. Players on those Cowboys teams were treated like stars everywhere they went in Dallas. Lincoln lived it up, got into drugs, and eventually lost control. Jen brought him to BHOP while I was down there, but we had really different experiences. While I was in the Seaside units, getting to go to the beach and having chefs cook my meals, Lincoln was in the main building, where it was more institutional, a place where the whole group lived under strict rules.

Randy was part of the group. And I agreed to take part, too.

Just as Randy and I needed to throw down whatever pain pills we had left before we got on our flights to Florida, Drew needed to fill up on his own poison one last time. He had a water bottle full of booze to keep him calm on the plane; this was after the $72 bar tab he ran up drinking martinis in the airport bar before boarding. Then, there was a bottle of rum for the ride to the Recovery Center, where we were waiting for him.

Despite Jen warning me about Drew's condition, he was so much worse than I expected. Drew had tried to go to rehab before, but it almost killed him and he left. He came to Florida not trusting anybody, especially doctors.

Drew's mother was there, too. It was his mother who had heard about P.A.S.T. and reached out to see if they could help her son. I saw her standing off to the side of the room, and I couldn't help but think of Cecy and the girls and what I'd put them through. I could see how helpless she felt; she couldn't help her son, and it was killing her. I didn't know what I could do to help Drew, but I knew I had to do everything I could to ease this woman's suffering.

It wasn't until I met Randy that I began to realize that I wasn't alone in my struggles. I wasn't the only guy out there with these issues. I wasn't the only former football player living in pain.

Being with Drew and Lincoln and Craig and Randy reinforced a lesson I have never forgotten: we are not alone. We might have different issues that we deal with in different ways. Drew fought the pain from his football injuries with alcohol. Randy and I took pills.

We are different but we are not alone.

You don't realize that when you're in addiction's grip. You're alone, a man in a hole, one you can't get out of alone. People reach down to try to help you, but you just can't reach their hands. So you stop trying. Then you slide further down the hole, where it's harder for anyone to reach you. Eventually you stop looking up for them.

But there is help out there. P.A.S.T. has provided more than $4.5 million worth of pro bono care for hundreds of retired professional athletes in need. Most of us came from the NFL, but there are baseball and basketball players, too.

We are not alone.

We don't start off as addicts. We start off playing a violent fucking sport. Taking medication so that we can play is part of the gig. So, we take the Vicodins they give us when we're hurt. We take the Ambien they give us to sleep. And we take the Toradol shots to make it through practice. Then, when we get out of the game and we still have pain—as we all do—we go to the doctor, except our tolerance is so high we need more meds than the average patient. What you may need one pill to handle, we need four.

We don't start out taking 1,400 pills a month. That's where we ended up.

We are not alone.

That's one of the first things I tell the guys now in my role as a peer counselor for P.A.S.T. I tell them that I was in the same place they're in. I thought I was alone. I thought I was helpless. I thought I was hopeless.

I tell them that I used to run around to get prescriptions from five different doctors, none of whom knew what the others were giving me. And they laugh because they know exactly what I'm talking about.

I tell them about the 1,400 pills a month. About how I had no idea there was anybody out there who could possibly know what I was going through—until I met Randy and found out he was taking 1,500. This always surprises them, to find out they aren't alone. They come to P.A.S.T. and immediately find out that they are among people who will not judge them. It's a lot easier to talk to like-minded people you can relate to. There are no reasons to hold anything back.

There is no reason for anyone to suffer in silence anymore.

You hear about guys like Junior Seau and Dave Duerson, guys who killed themselves because of the struggles they were having. Both guys were dealing with the effects of chronic traumatic encephalopathy—CTE—a degenerative brain disease associated with head injuries. You hear about guys like Corwin Brown, a safety I played with in New England and with the Jets. Corwin was a great guy and a good Christian man; I don't think I ever heard him curse. In 2011, he held his own family hostage at gunpoint in their house. He shot himself after a seven-hour standoff with police. He survived. But his defense during the trial was that he was mentally unstable as a result of the head injuries he suffered during his NFL career.

I hear stories like theirs and it breaks my heart. It's fucking tragic. What if somebody could have sat down with Corwin Brown or Junior Seau or Dave Duerson and said, "I'm struggling, too"? How many stories are there of guys in desperate situations who we never hear about?

I don't want to hear any more stories like theirs. Junior Seau played 20 years in the NFL. He'll be a first-ballot Hall of Famer. How deep a hole was he in to take his own life?

Believe me, I know the answer. I understand what these guys must have been thinking. At one point, I was thinking it, too.

This is the only way out.

I see some of the older football players and the shit they're dealing with, and it terrifes me. Early onset dementia. Parkinson's. Is that what I'm going to be dealing with when I'm 50? If I'm shitting in my pants and I don't know it, I would think the same thing—it's time to ride the bullet. That's not living. It's barely even surviving.

Players need to know that there are people out there who care and who can help them. Guys do get their lives back.

Drew Macfarlan got clean. So did Lincoln Coleman. Craig Sauer got married recently. Randy Grimes is a community liaison for BHOP. Ray Lucas is still here.

We can come out the other side.

Take Charlie Brown, the two-time Pro Bowl receiver for the Redskins. He caught a touchdown in Super Bowl XVII. Charlie suffered close to 10 concussions in his six-year NFL career, and saw little blue stars flashing in front of his eyes after every one of them. And he never said a word.

Years after he was out of the game, Charlie started forgetting things. He was coaching football at Savannah High School in Georgia, came home from practice one day, and couldn't remember his sister-in-law's name. He had to call his wife to find out.

He started forgetting the names of his students, his players. It got so bad that he had to quit his coaching job. Charlie had to wear sunglasses everywhere he went, because lights—even basic indoor lighting—would trigger unbearable headaches.

Charlie came to P.A.S.T. shortly after I did. After years of working with the doctors, he got his life back. He returned to coaching. When he spoke at a fund-raising dinner in New Jersey a few nights before Super Bowl XLVIII was played down the road in MetLife Stadium, Charlie wore his glasses at the podium. Regular glasses.

Christian Okoye spoke at that same event. He called for a new "season of openness," where football players no longer feel obligated to keep quiet about the injuries they suffer.

Christian kept quiet about his own suffering for decades. Until Super Bowl week in 2014, he hadn't talked much about the worst concussion of his career. Then he ran into Richard Dent, the Hall of Fame defensive end—and the guy involved in the hit that caused his worst concussion.

Christian and Dent started discussing the play, how Christian was running to his left, bounced the play outside, and saw Dent right in his path. Knowing no other way to get yardage, Christian did his thing—he lowered his head, braced for impact, and hit Dent as hard as he could. Dent was braced, too; guys tended to clench up when the Nigerian Nightmare was bearing down on them. Dent countered by launching into Christian as hard as he could.

Until they met all these years later, Christian Okoye never knew that on the same play he suffered the worst concussion of his NFL career, he also dealt Richard Dent the worst concussion of his career.

And, of course, when that play was over, both players went straight back to their huddles, even though Christian's right side was numb and he couldn't see out of his right eye. Neither even considered going to the sideline or mentioning it to their trainers afterward. After all, they had been told throughout their entire playing careers, it was just a "ding."

Now, Christian's dealing with the aftermath of those "dings." His neck surgery was a success, although he still has trouble with his balance. But his hands tremble sometimes. He gets muscle tremors. He is getting tested for early signs of dementia or Parkinson's. He's not keeping it to himself anymore. He's getting help.

Richie Anderson is getting help. After years of suffering alone, of being embarrassed to talk to anyone about what he was going through, Richie's seeing his doctor a few times a month, getting treatments for the concussions he suffered during his career. He doesn't know how many of them there were—at least 10, including a couple where he was knocked unconscious. He's seen the stars, the sparkling lights in front of his eyes that he can't blink away. He's had the memory loss; one day, he couldn't remember the name of his nephew.

He suffered from depression, just like I did, and left the game before he was ready. Richie's NFL career also ended because of a neck injury. His problems began during the 2001 season, when he was still with the Jets; I had already moved on to Miami. Richie was on the kickoff return unit and was trying to set up Mike Vrabel for a sneak block. But Vrabel didn't buy the fake. Instead, he went straight at Richie, his helmet smashing into the left side of Richie's chin.

When the play was over and the adrenaline had subsided, Richie felt a fireball hit him in the back of his neck. But he never said anything to the trainers or the coaches. He kept playing.

For the rest of that season and three more afterward.

Christian Okoye played three seasons after hurting his neck. I would've kept playing forever after my neck injury, if someone would've let me.

Finally, the pain in Richie's neck and head got so bad he was forced to have two vertebrae, C5 and C6, fused. He had just finished his second season with the Cowboys after landing there in 2003, the same year Bill Parcells arrived as head coach; Richie Anderson was a classic Parcells Guy. His second season ended early when he was put on injured reserve before Week 14. The papers said he was out with a "pinched nerve."

During a follow-up visit, doctors took an X-ray of Richie's neck to check the progress of his recovery. At that point, Richie was still contemplating whether to return for a 13th NFL season or move into coaching. Then, the doctor came into the room, slid the films up on the light board, and saw the look of fear on Richie's face.

"That's my neck?" Richie asked. He knew right away it was over.

He went to meet with Parcells and described what he saw in the X-rays.

"I'm not going to let you play with that. Even if you want to," Parcells told him.

Richie retired in April 2005. It took eight years for him to seek help. He's finally getting treatment for things he couldn't bring himself to talk to his family about, let alone a doctor.

There are way too many stories like this. And still guys think they are alone.

How could you possibly be alone when more than 4,800 former players were part of a class action lawsuit against the NFL? I was one of those players.

Two writers from the *Washington Times*, Nathan Fenno and Luke Rosiak, compiled a master list of all the plaintiffs involved in what everybody knows as "the NFL Concussion Suit." It's pretty striking to go online and scroll through all the names on that list. I'm one of 116 quarterbacks on the list. One of 276 guys who played for the Jets. One of 1,034 guys who played between six and nine seasons in the league. I see the names of teammates, guys I threw the ball to, guys I handed the ball to, guys who ate Cecy's chicken parm at my house on Thursday nights. I see guys on the list I played against in college and in the NFL. Probably even some guys who caused a couple of my concussions.

The day in August 2013 that the NFL agreed to settle the suit for $765 million, I got a text from those lawyers.

"We won the suit," it said.

I texted them back right away.

"Do I get any money?"

The answer I got was not encouraging: "Eventually, yes."

But the point of the lawsuit was never about the money. Don't get me wrong—we could use the money. My family is nowhere near all the way back financially. We wouldn't be in the house we're in today if my parents hadn't loaned us money for the down payment. If someone wanted to give me $5 today, I'm taking it.

Still, if someone were to ask me, "Would you rather have the money or the knowledge?" I would take the knowledge. I just want to know what the NFL knows. I want to know what's coming for me.

The lawyers called the lawsuit a victory. But what did we, the players, really get out of it? The NFL didn't tell us anything. We could have learned so much from the studies they might have done over the years. But we settled and we didn't find out shit.

Knowledge is the key to all of this. Dave Duerson knew it. That's why he wanted his brain examined after his death. He shot himself in the chest so that his brain could be studied. It was donated to a place at Boston University called the Center for the Study of Traumatic Encephalopathy, which has been studying CTE since 2008. But when the lawsuit was settled—when we "won"—the NFL didn't have to disclose anything it had learned before that. What did the league know, and when did it know it? We'll probably never find out.

But players, active and retired, need to know as much as we can. That's why I've gotten involved with Dr. Focazio's newest program, Eternity Medicine, which has evolved out of P.A.S.T. It's a preventative approach to treating the problems that are probably coming, not a reactive one. At P.A.S.T., they fix the problems that we already have. Preventative medicine aims to find out everything we can as far in advance as we can, so that we can predict, slow down, and maybe even totally eliminate potential medical issues before they become problems.

Eternity Medicine measured 250 markers in my blood; they discovered that my arteries were hardening and that I was a borderline diabetic. We were able to take steps to help me avoid full-blown diabetes.

The tests also told me that my testosterone was ridiculously low. A normal man in his forties should have a testosterone count of about 800 to 1,000 nanograms per deciliter. Mine was down to 600. I took opiates for so long that my body had stopped making testosterone. When you take downers for three years, your pituitary gland figures it can stop monitoring things like testosterone—obviously you're not using it, lying around the bed for days at a time.

My test results indicated what kind of supplements I needed to be taking, things like fish oil, which improves cognitive functioning for people suffering from head trauma. All of this is about improving my quality of life going forward. Because I have a lot of shit left to do that I want to be able to remember. I have three girls to walk down the aisle.

I'm already dealing with the damage done to my brain. I have moments when I know what I want to say but the words don't want to come out.

I'm color-blind now. My blues are grays, my browns are blues. Which is a problem, because I still like to look good—it's a quarterback thing. Now, I have to check with Cecy before I walk out of the house to make sure I'm not dressed like Ronald McDonald. Socks are the biggest problem. I put them on, make sure they match, go to the studio, and realize that I'm wearing blue socks with a brown suit. The fucking colors keep changing on me.

I am starting to forget things. There are times when I can't remember what I did the day before, times when my wife sends me out to ShopRite and I've forgotten what I'm supposed to buy before I even get to the parking lot. My family has caught me a couple of times frozen in front of the fridge, just staring at the shelves. They ask me what I'm looking for, and I have no idea.

I will do whatever it takes to delay the process as long as I can. Because I've seen what's coming.

And, let's be honest, the NFL needs to do more, too. The league is making $10 billion a year; it needs to do more to help the guys who built the league into the unparalleled success it is today.

There's been some progress. The league is evolving. And that's a good thing.

I like how they're trying to take care of receivers downfield. Believe me, I hung out my share of guys over the middle during my career; they need to be protected when they're in defenseless positions. The best way to treat concussions is to stop them before they happen. Make no mistake—they are unavoidable in football. Head injuries are inevitable in a collision sport where you have 300-pound guys who run a 4.5/40 smashing into each other. But I think the league is right in trying to minimize the opportunities for one to happen.

I like that the league is protecting the quarterback. What people want to see is high-scoring games with lots of passing. They want to see Tom Brady, coming back in the final minute, down by four with no timeouts left. When I was playing, quarterbacks were live targets; you could drill a quarterback in his back and not worry about a penalty.

I like that there are concussion tests on the sideline, and that doctors and trainers will take a player's helmet away so he can't go back in the game before he's cleared. They're trying to protect players from themselves, because players—even with all we know now about the long-term effects of head injuries—aren't going to change.

It's who we are. You cannot play the game of football if you're thinking about getting hurt or consciously trying to avoid injury. If you mentally acknowledge that you're going to wind up having this many surgeries or suffer this sort of permanent damage, you're finished. That would be a display of weakness, and football is a world where weakness dooms you. The weak sink. You have to believe, to your fucking core, that you are stronger than your opponent is, that you are more determined than he is, that nothing can stop you. You have to be invincible—or at least act like you are.

As long as that remains a fundamental part of a football player's mentality—and it always will be—painkillers will remain a part of the NFL. Forever. Period. It's a violent sport, and players need medicine to get them through the things that otherwise will sabotage their careers.

But the NFL must do a better job of taking care of its players when the lights go out. The lights will go out on everybody, and none of us are ready when it happens.

I thought I was going to play forever. Then one day, it's over. You get your black garbage bag, a kick in the balls, and a "Have a nice day." There's no exit strategy, especially for the guys who don't make $6 million a year—which is most of us in the NFL. There's a huge misconception that everyone in the game is a millionaire. Only a handful of guys on a team make set-for-life money. Everyone else is facing several decades of working another job.

It really shouldn't be that hard for the billion-dollar machine to do more for its players at the end of their careers. At the very least, there are two simple things the NFL should do to better prepare players for life on the other side of the game.

First, every time a team gives you the black garbage bag to pack up all your shit, it should also hand you a sheet of paper with five phone numbers in it. They would be the contact numbers for players to call if they find themselves in dire straits.

One could be the number for a counselor, someone for them to talk to about the transition. Because, let's face it, none of the guys in the league are used to life as an ordinary Moe. Depression starts to creep in when guys can't acclimate to a life after the lights go out.

There could be numbers of former players who can be a resource for newly retired players. The sooner guys understand that they are not alone in the world, the better.

There could be numbers for places like P.A.S.T. and Eternity Medicine, or any other programs that will help players deal with the physical and psychological challenges they are going to face. And they are all going to face something.

And there could be a number for someone who can help these guys get a job. I know the NFL preaches about preparing for the future at the rookie symposium when young players first get to the league. But no one in that room is listening. You're talking about the long-term effects of injuries, the importance of saving money, and preparing for a career after football to a bunch of bulletproof 22-year-olds who are convinced they are going to play and live forever. No kid in that room thinks any bad shit is ever going to happen to him.

I have news for them. It will.

They are going to have to go to work when they're done with football. And it would certainly be helpful if the NFL provided a more direct connection to players already out in the working world.

The NFL could also make a real difference with health insurance. The guys who play a certain number of years in the NFL should have medical coverage for the rest of their lives. How hard would that be? I know it wouldn't be cheap, but why shouldn't the NFL take care of all the players who have ever played the game by making sure they have insurance?

We give everything to football. And our insurance runs out before we realize just how much damage was done, before we know how big our problems really are.

If I had not lost my insurance after five years, I could have had the disc replacement surgery in my neck when I needed it. All that shit I lived through afterward quite possibly could have been avoided. I might not have been in pain all those years. I might never have become addicted to painkillers. I might never have gotten to the point where I had a plan to kill myself.

That's what really bothers me. For the money it would have cost the NFL to extend my insurance policy, I might not have gone through the hell that I did. And all the shit I put my body through with the pain pills—everything I put my family through—could have possibly been avoided. I see all the guys who come to P.A.S.T. because they have nowhere else to turn, and it upsets me. So many of their struggles could have been avoided.

I'm not big on what-ifs, but it's impossible not to think that way sometimes. What if my insurance hadn't run out? What if somebody had been there for me to talk to? For Dave Duerson to talk to? For Junior Seau to talk to?

Why should it be so hard for the NFL to do the right thing? Guys like me are willing to do whatever it takes to stay in the league for as long as we can. Even if it's just running down to cover kicks on special teams, we risk it all for the chance to play the greatest game in the world on its biggest stage.

Our reward should be simple. The NFL should say, "If, god forbid, anything happens to you, you're covered. Physically, mentally, whatever you're going through, we've set this money—from the billions you helped earn for us—aside for you, and for everyone like you."

Because here's the thing—we love the game of football.

None of us blame football for what happened to us. Christian Okoye doesn't. Joe Klecko doesn't. Randy Grimes doesn't. Richie Anderson doesn't. I don't.

I love football. I miss it every single day.

I have been out of the game for more than 10 years, and it's still the first thing I think about when I wake up in the morning. Every damn day.

I miss the locker room. There's shit that goes on in there you just don't find anywhere else in the world. I had a ball in there.

I miss the camaraderie, the us-against-them, all-for-one mentality. You put in all the blood, sweat, and tears, go through all the off-season workouts, battle back from injuries, just so you could be part of it. You cross that white line together and you are out there with your brothers. Eleven together are strong. One dies, all die.

I miss the adrenaline, the feeling that comes from preparing for that one moment, and then stepping out on that field and doing to the other guy what I know I'm capable of. And that there's nothing he can do to stop me. I loved the whole "Let me at 'em" fever you get when you're in the tunnel.

When I was a kid, I would be so excited on game day, my body would be buzzing. I almost couldn't handle all the excitement. From Pop Warner through college, I threw up five minutes before every game; I was like a volcano inside. I couldn't wait to get out there and hit something.

I miss the game.

Even in the mornings, when waking up is so hard, when I hear all the creaking and the cracking in my knees and my neck, when it takes me 20 minutes to get out of bed. Even on the days when I have trouble turning my head, days when I feel those speed bumps up and down the muscles in my back.

I miss football.

Now that I'm clear, I probably miss it more than I ever did before. I'll pop in a DVD of a game I played in, and all those emotions come flooding back. Or somebody will start talking to me about a game or a play that they remember from my career, and my insides will start revving. I love it.

I have just one regret about my football career: I wish I had appreciated it more while it was happening.

I enjoyed it all, having Cecy and my parents and my sister and my boys there, for them to drive six minutes to the stadium to see me play quarterback in the NFL. I enjoyed seeing the Lucas jerseys.

But I wish I had appreciated it more while it was happening. Because it was Fantasyland.

Even if they told me back then, "Ray, you're going to go through back surgery and three neck surgeries and elbow surgery and four knee surgeries," I would have signed up for it all. Just for the chance to be part of the game.

They told me that if I kept playing with my back as bad as it was, I could end up in a wheelchair. I didn't hesitate: I kept playing.

As broke as my body is, as much pain as I'm still in, if they called me tomorrow and said, "We need you to cover kickoffs," I would be there.

In a fucking heartbeat.

We're football players. And I don't blame the game for what we're going through. The game gave us so much.

It taught us about discipline. Teamwork. Sacrifice. Hard work. Dedication. That no individual is bigger than the team. These are all things we learned through playing football, all things we all need to learn to succeed in life.

It bothers me when I hear parents worrying about whether they should allow their sons to play football. Do they know that a study reported in 2013 that the highest catastrophic injury rate in sports occurs in cheerleading? No one's talking about boycotting cheerleading.

I would never tell other parents whether they should let their sons play football. As the father of three daughters, it's not something that I've ever had to consider from a parent's perspective.

But I will.

For almost a year now, my family has been trying to adopt a son. We went through all the classes, 9-to-5 every day in Jersey City for five weeks in a row. We participated in a battery of extensive interviews, including one-on-ones with my girls. We were open and honest about everything we'd been through, about my injuries, about my addiction. We showed them all the love we have in our home, and we showed them our commitment as a family to providing some young man all the love he can handle.

We did the home inspections, made sure we added all the smoke detectors and carbon monoxide detectors to be up to code. And in December 2013, we were certified. Cleared. We were given the green light to adopt a boy.

To adopt Michael.

When we started the process, they directed us to the AdoptUSKids website. Cecy found Michael, a seven-year-old boy in North Carolina. She and the girls would go online and look at his picture. I wouldn't look, not until we knew for sure.

It's a long, frustrating process, and I understand why that is. If they have 10 people trying to find a home for each of these kids, they're 20 people short of what they need. Still, it's hard. We thought we might be able to start visiting him before Christmas, but that didn't happen. Then, we heard that we were one of 30 families inquiring about Michael.

But I have faith that God is going to give us our son at the right time. That eventually we're going to have a little man in the house. Someone we can shower with love. Someone I can blame for leaving the toilet seat up—it's impossible for me to get away with it, living with my four women.

Cecy teases me sometimes.

"What if he wants to play the piano and not sports?"

"That's fine. We'll send him back."

I'm joking, of course. If he wants to play the piano, he'll play the piano. If he wants to be a brainiac, he'll be a brainiac.

And if he wants to play football, he'll play football.

If he wants to get down and dirty, I'll enroll him in Football 101, taught by his father.

Football is a part of my life and always will be. It's something I will always love. It just doesn't define me anymore. It's who I was. It's what I did.

But it's not who I am today.

Today, I'm Ray Lucas, Jersey boy from Harrison. Rutgers class of 1996. I'm a retired football player. I'm a former quarterback. I'm a broadcaster. I'm a peer counselor.

I'm an addict. Every day I wake up in pain, and every day I fight through pain, and every day I fight to stay clean.

And every day, I'm trying to be the best son, the best friend, the best brother, the best father, and the best husband I can be. Whatever it takes.

For me, the game is over.

But I have the rest of my life to live.

Acknowledgments

RAY would like to thank Bill Parcells, Dr. Focazio and Debra, Dr. McInerney, Dr. Emami, Dr. Lattuga, Dr. Patel, Dr. Battaglia, Jennifer Smith, J.R. Conrad, "The Boyz" (Jason "Rooster" Czwakiel, Mike "Post" Gilmore, Jack "Paper" Nicosia, Michael Rowe, Lance "Black" Haynes, Mike "Larry Love" Oeckel, Keith Lodge, Ronnie Greenmier, Joe Carr, and Sergio Tigliero), Vinny "Pasta" Testaverde, Richie Anderson, Jason Ferguson, Wayne Chrebet, Glenn Foley, Pepper Johnson, William Roberts, Dan Henning, Dedric Ward, Isaac Solotaroff, BHOP and its staff, Dr. Lukens, Dr. Rosenblatt, Olga and Anthony Capoaso, Joe Tanchina, Jim Halpin, Al Ruiz, Charles "Chuckie Love" Comprelli, Patti Gerris, Nick Landy, Jaime Denman, Jack Denman, Camp Fatima, Vinny Ferriero, Ronnie Catrombone, Uncle Jack Rodgers, Uncle Mike Rodgers, Aunt Penny Johnson, Coach Lloyd Splane, Coach Franny Falvine, Coach Joe Choffo, Coach Pete Falvine, Coach Alan Doffant, Coach Bill Hartman, Coach Larry Manning, Coach Ralph Borgess, Coach Richie Howell, Kevin Barber, Coach Doug Graber, Coach Stan Parish, Coach Mose Rison, Bruce Presley, Curtis Tribbitt, Marco Battaglia, Earl Simmons, Wes Bridges, Rutgers Football, Rutgers University, Tim Pernetti, Jason Baum, Chris Carlin,

Brian Higgins, Kevin Higgins, Mike Roberts, Richie Roberts, the Mesa Family, my agent, Mark Lepselter, Pastor Terry Smith and TLCC Church, and, of course, Mom, Dad, Alicen, Clara, Cecy, Rayven, Madison, and Kayla.

David would like to thank his family, Elizabeth, Maia, Dylan, Susan, Barry, Carol Ann, and George, for their support and encouragement.

Many thanks to Adam Motin, Noah Amstadter, Tom Bast, Mitch Rogatz, and everyone at Triumph Books who helped us share this important story.

About the Authors

RAY LUCAS played seven seasons in the NFL as a quarterback and special teams player for the New England Patriots, New York Jets, Miami Dolphins, and Baltimore Ravens. He is an analyst covering the Jets for SNY New York and a color analyst for the Rutgers Radio Network. He lives in Harrison, New Jersey, with his wife, Cecy, and their three daughters, Rayven, Madison, and Kayla.

DAVID SEIGERMAN is a veteran sports journalist whose writing career began in newspapers (*Newsday, Jackson Sun*) and moved on to magazines (*College Sports Magazine*). In 1996 he moved from print to broadcast media, becoming a field producer for CNN/SI and eventually the managing editor at College Sports Television. Since 2003, he has been a freelance writer and producer, and co-wrote and co-produced the feature-length documentary, *The Warrior Ethos: The Experience and Tradition of Boxing at West Point.* He is also the co-author of the best-selling *Take Your Eye Off the Ball: How to Watch Football by Knowing Where to Look* with NFL analyst Pat Kirwan. He lives in New York with his wife, Elizabeth, and their two children.